www.united-pc.eu

Lisa Biritz

The Opening

Dolphins, Whales and Star Beings –
A Journey Home

Foreword and Cover Painting by
Francene Hart

Contents

For Star and Rose

Whirling out from the womb of the cosmos, energy is the most basic stuff of creation.

Love is the key that unlocks this language and helps us more fully realize our divinity.

See yourself flying on the wings of universal love and experience the freedom of knowing you are never separate but are truly an integral part of the divine order.

Francene Hart

Foreword

When I met Lisa, I immediately recognized a woman of vision and integrity. Her gentle direct manner impressed me as a seeker who has allowed synchronicity and openhearted curiosity to guide her spiritual path.

Reading this book, I sometimes felt she was telling my own story. Travel and the exploration of transcendent guidance from both real and unseen realms have taught me to trust and listen. Our cetacean friends and star beings have also been my teachers.

It is only natural that my painting *Swimming with Dolphins* graces the cover of Lisa´s book.

Lisa's *Opening* and subsequent adventures provide the reader with a look at a woman who has followed her heart and divine guidance, is living that truth and sharing it with grace. This book gently tells us her amazing story; the reader experiences the beauty and magic with her.

It is an honor to read the words of one who knows her life's purpose and has actively engaged her passion. *The Opening* is an expansive account of a great life adventure and a gift to us all.

Aloha,

Francene Hart
Visionary Artist, Hawaii
www.FranceneHart.com

1. The Opening

Oceans, covering almost three quarters of our blue planet's surface. Dolphins leaping and surfing the waves. Huge gentle whales diving down deep. Thousands of tiny yellow fish create an own being. Bright orange and red coral – home for millions of living beings.

Mountain rivers with rainbow trout and pink-colored pebbles. Transparent, cool water splashing downwards. Tall oaks and pines, the smell of sap in the air. Pure, fresh air. A falcon's cry, invisible to the eye, so high up. A deer appears, grazes, big ears and dark eyes listen and look attentively.

By the time I am 30 – having gone through numerous experiences with employers -, I come to the conclusion that my only boss on this planet is the Earth herself. Earth gives me a home, food and clothing. I talk to her, ask her questions. She answers. Sometimes, she talks to me without my asking her. I do what she tells me, follow her guidance; nobody else's.

The universe created heaven and Earth, not heaven and hell.

Trees as high as buildings, lush green leafy roofs. Monkeys holler, leap through branches. Iridescent butterflies the size of a hand. Hot, humid air. Flowers and plants of all shapes, colors and smells. Purple frogs glowing in the dark.

Villages and cities with town squares and statues of past history. Markets with people from all over the world selling and buying, talking and looking. Handcrafted clothing and fabrics. Tables full of fruit and vegetable. Children running and laughing.

It is such a miracle and wonder – this planet. So much beauty.

Aside from Earth, I also talk with other beings: angels, animal guides, fairies and nature beings, spirit entities, star family and spiritual teachers. Not to forget the dolphins and whales. Nowadays communicating with them is second nature.

In my childhood it is natural, too. But growing up in an environment that doesn´t support this, I lose this ability for a decade. It doesn´t return until I am in my early twenties. That is when the opening – or should I say re-opening – begins.

I call these events »openings«, because they are exactly that: opening up to more than the eye can see - to the invisible world.

The visible world is what we can see: stones, plants, animals, people and everything humans have created on Earth. The invisible world is what flows and pulsates behind all this; the soul of everything. It is what makes life as we know it take place – where we come from when we are born and where we return to when we die. The Hawaiian *Huna*-tradition calls this life force *mana*, the Yogis of India name this energy *prana*. It also includes many beings and spirit entities, there to help and guide us. That has been their job for aeons.

My first opening happens while I am in Namibia on a two-week assignment for the women´s magazine *marie claire*. I am researching for an article about the relationship between Caucasians and Coloreds there since the land´s independence from South Africa in 1990. Accompanying me is a photographer, himself a white South African. On the way there on our long flight, he tells me his story: that he is in the army by the time he is 18 years against the freedom fighters in Namibia. After only a short period, he is struck by lightning – and survives. This experience literally en-lightens him. It wakes him up to what he is actually doing there: fighting in an inhumane war. He awakens from the craziness of any war. After his reconvalescence he moves to Europe to become a photographer and filmmaker.

We travel all over the country, driving endless miles, visiting numerous people and sites. I am fascinated by the country´s vastness. Sometimes we stop the car in the middle of nowhere. We get out, silence, in the desert. In the far distance a lonely tall tree – or is it a giraffe? Flimmering heat. Nothingness.

After a week I forget to wear my hat. We are in a wildlife reserve, staying in luxurious tents with carpets and beds. By the evening I have a high fever: severe sun stroke. I throw up dinner and manage, with the help of the photographer, to get back to my tent. He gives me electrolytes, waits to make sure I drink a lot before leaving me for the night.

I am in a delirium. I hear sounds outside the tent, animals. Exhausted, I sleep.

I wake up, shivering. I see an antilope standing in my tent. I know it cannot be real, I see the tent flaps closed. Yet there it is. I take my waterglass, to make sure I am not in a dream. I am not, I can drink. I see the antilope. It gazes at me steadily. It is very beautiful. I feel a warm and pleasant tingling spread all over my body as it looks at me.

Suddenly the antilope changes its shape and turns into a tiny, old man. He is wearing nothing but a small loincloth. He appears ancient and must be at least a head shorter than I. He smiles gently. Then he walks over to me and carefully rubs my head, massaging and holding it, for a minute or so. He leaves.

I fall into a deep sleep.

The next morning, I wake up with a headache. The fever is gone. It is lunchtime, I go to the dining room. I meet the photographer. He is surprised to already see me on my feet. I tell him I feel fine, adding jokingly that I dreamt I was healed by an antilope that turned into a little old man. He gives me an intense look and asks me to tell him what happened. »You were being helped by what sounds like a Bushman spirit. Or a Bushman«, he says.

He explains to me that the Bushmen are the indigenous people of the southern African countries, living in tribes in the desert. »They are the only ones who can live here without the help of technology. They practice their own shamanism.« I have never heard this word before and look at the photographer questioningly. »They are able to heal with the energy flow of nature and the universe«, he explains.

I am fascinated by the concept that everything is one, is connected. That we are all sparks from the same light, the same source; that which people call God. That there are healers who are able to shapeshift into animals - like maybe the Bushman did into an antilope to come and help me so that I would recover soon to carry on for the research of my article.

I ask the photographer why he knows all this. He tells me that he had a similar experience after he was struck by lightning: »I am convinced the Bushmen or Bushmen spirits saved my life. After that, I started researching their ways. In the process, I discovered what was really inside me, my true being. You know«, he says looking at my intently, »you´re not only about what you look like, what sex you are and how you were raised. You´re about your true life´s calling. What you came here for. Your unique, one of a kind cosmic blueprint.«

We have just a few days left and continue on our assignment. On one particular day, we meet a hitchhiker at a restaurant. We give him a lift to the next larger town, several hours away. He is Australian, beaming and handsome, about my age – I am 23 at the time. He says he has been traveling for over a year, after completing his college studies. He wants to travel the world before returning home and getting a job.

I enjoy his presence, his friendly and relaxed demeanor. He is interesting to talk and listen to. I think to myself that I would also love to travel the world with a backpack.

Upon returning home, I can't get this idea out of my head. Even though I have a top-notch job as assistant editor for *marie claire* with a promising career ahead – the pull onward is stronger. So I decide to quit and just do it: travel the world with a backpack. I have always been a good student, started university with 17, graduate *magna cum laude* second best of my class with 500 students, editor-in-chief of the university newspaper. I am confident that I will get a job again, upon returning from my world travels.

Six months later I have saved up enough money to last me a year on a backpacker's budget. I sell most of what I own and cancel all my insurances, even my health insurance. I want to be free as a bird and just fly through life for a while. No responsibilities, no strings attached.

I decide to start in Asia, in the Himalayas. From there I will travel all around the world. So my first stop is Bhutan, where my second opening happens.

2. Ministry of Happiness

I am lying in my tent, resting. Singhi, my guide, is outside preparing a meal over the fire. We have been hiking all day. It is dark outside, the sun has already set.

»Lisa, come here«, I hear Singhi. I crawl out of my tent, thinking he is calling me for dinner. He is standing with his back to the fire. I walk over to him. »Look«, he says, pointing at the mountain. I look up and see a shimmering light, as if it were dusk. But it is already dark outside. »Something is shining«, I say. »Look again«, he replies, »but not the normal way. See through your eyes as if you were feeling what is there. Use your Third Eye.«

I squint, trying hard to do what he tells me. I have no idea what he means with looking through the Third Eye, even though I know what it is since arriving in Bhutan. It is depicted prominently as a dot between the eyebrows of the saints on all the paintings here. Singhi watches me and laughs. »Just relax«, he says, turning back to whatever the shimmering light is.

I close my eyes and try it differently this time. First, I feel through my Third Eye. I sense something is there. I then slowly open my eyes, trying not to focus. There is still the shimmering light. And then, something very odd. They look like big balls of light, glowing.

»Big balls of light?« I ask Singhi, to make sure we are seeing the same thing. »Yes«, he answers, »they are moving around each other and in different colors.«

Apparently we are seeing the same thing. »What is that?«, I ask.

»They are from the other world«, he replies.

I am shocked by his matter-of-fact statement. I watch the lightballs twirling up and down the mountainside, gliding quickly, then slowing down to a halt. They are rotating around one another, beautifully. It looks like they are dancing.

I have never seen anything like this before. Maybe they are ball lightning? I remember learning at school that ball lightning usually do not last longer than a second. But these are still there and many, maybe a dozen. They are moving in all directions now, up and down, left and right. At all speeds, from very fast to complete standstill. They also have different colors, glowing gold, light silver, pastel pink, green. They are vibrant, glowing.

We watch silently until they move farther and farther away. Up and to the side of the mountain, a gigantic Himalayan peak. Until they are mere tiny dots – and then gone. Just like eagles soaring high into the sky – at some point they simply disappear to the human eye.

I ask Singhi: »What do you mean they are from the other world?« Over our simple fireside dinner, he explains. There is a firm belief in the spirit world in Bhutan. People have an understanding about life and death - where they come from when they are born and where they return to when they die. It is commonly accepted knowledge that the souls of those deceased exist somewhere else as spirits, before they reincarnate again on Earth - or elsewhere in the universe or even in parallel dimensions.

The Kingdom of Bhutan, which is a small country about the size of Switzerland, is jointly governed by state and church. Their Buddhist church is similar to that in Tibet and firmly believes in reincarnation. Humans reincarnate as often as necessary until they have learned their lessons to become loving and enlightened beings. That is what karma is; returning until the slate is clean.

I remember the movie *Groundhog Day*. In it, the main character repeats the same day over and over thousands of times. He always wakes up in the morning, never makes it to the next day because he is rude, unfriendly, hard to get along with. By the end of the movie, he has transformed into a friendly, caring and loving person. Then, finally, the next day comes. He is ready to move on to the next level. Singhi, who studied in the West, knows the movie and laughs. »Yes, kind of like that.«

One of the main goals of the Bhutanese government is that the country's people feel happy about life. Happiness is, next to health and education, the main national agenda. They actually have an official Ministry of Happiness, headed by a member of the royal family.

»It is part of our religion«, says Singhi, »that happiness is more worthwhile than all the riches and temptations of life.« He tells me about his years in the United States, where he saw so much material wealth but so little inner peace and happiness. He thinks many people confuse material wealth with true happiness, which can only come from within. He was glad to return home, to Bhutan, after he completed his studies.

The Ministry of Happiness conducts surveys all over the country to find out in which regions the people are happy and in which not. They use statistical methods of questioning for this. In those areas where happiness is low, the ministry seeks out the cause and attempts to solve it – regardless if it is a material or personal problem. Everybody is relieved if it is a material problem, because that is – according to their world view - only minor and can be taken care of. It is never the source of true happiness, but merely for temporary comfort and pleasure.

More difficult is solving the soul´s unhappiness. Then the ministry brings in Buddhist teachers as well as traditional healers. It is believed that if a person is unhappy or ill, it is a reflectioin of an imbalance in the entire community. In order to help the person, they have to heal the village. Therefore in the work done to an individual, sometimes the entire town is also present.

That evening, I sit by myself under the velvet sky, Singhi already asleep.

Millions of stars, trillions. Our Milky Way glows. There is so much we humans don't know and never will. Everything is a great mystery, we can never fully understand and grasp it. This realization relaxes me. I breathe deeply. It is indeed a mystery – a beautiful one. And I am part of it, an atom in it. I think about what Singhi told me earlier: »You are a spirit in a body on Earth.«

As I sit here, with no job agendas or appointments and all the time in the world, I realize there has to be more to life than getting up in the morning and going to your job. I start remembering. Experiences as a child and young teenager with angels, with my ancestors, even with star beings. They were always here; I just forgot.

I laugh. There is no way I can write about the lightball-spirits for the magazine. Shortly before I left on my trip, the editor-in-chief asked me to compose a series about my world travels. If I write about this, they will think I am crazy – or on drugs, hallucinating. Neither is the case. I will have to stick to writing about the usual tourist experiences for them – but nonetheless continue on my personal journey of opening up to the other side of the veil.

3. Love Force

More unusual things happen on my journey through Bhutan. One night, we stay in a travel lodge. It is large and in a remote area, on the outskirts of a small village. Most houses are without electricity and look ancient. Everything, including the people, appear medieval to me.

We are not alone in the travel lodge. A very large group of monks is also there. The thick smell of incense perfumes the air. The monks look magnificent in their dark red and yellow colored robes, sitting and meditating in what appears to be the lodge´s large communal and dining hall. I am surprised that they are not in a monastery. Singhi explains: "They are traveling to their winter monastery, like every year. With them is a high Lama, a spiritual teacher. In this area there is no monastery large enough to accommodate them all for the night on their trip."

That night, I barely close an eye. There is a constant squealing and screeching outside the walls of the lodge. It is very spooky and if I wouldn´t know any better, I would think there are a bunch of ghosts out there trying to get in.

At about one at night I can´t stand the noise anymore. I wander out into the hallway to wake up

Singhi in his room and ask him what's going on. To my surprise, I see a small group of monks down the hallway in the communal room. I walk towards them; their presence is comforting to me. As I come closer, I hear them reciting mantras - prayers. I sit down at a bit of a distance, because I know women are not allowed to approach monks. I relax into the mantras. The humminglike tone of their voices is very soothing.

I wake up from one of the monks gently pulling my sleeve. »You can go back to bed«, he says in clear English, »they have gone.« I look at him sleepy and confused. »Where there is light, there is dark. Polarity. The duality on earth.« He pauses as I stare at him; not because he is talking to me, but because he sounds like a distinguished university professor. I notice that his robes are colored differently than those of the other monks. Then I realize: He is the Lama.

»Those are spirits of the deceased gone astray«, he explains. »They are nothing but our other side. So we love them also, in compassion and understanding. They are often there where we go, wanting to have our light. We pray for them to find the true light on their path again and help to guide them there.«

»Are they dangerous? What can I do to protect myself?« I ask nervously.

He smiles. »Don't worry – they can't harm you. Just tell them that you are not the source of light – that it is the big light and love they must return and travel to. That is the strongest protection. Love and light. Surround yourself in love, feel love and compassion in and through yourself for yourself and all beings.«

To this day, I use this simple but highly effective protection the Buddhist Lama taught me that night. No special spells or mixtures – just love, compassion and light. It is the most potent medicine there is. The elemental and ancient power which nourishes all of life is forevermore love. Love is the strongest force there is; it is the glue holding the universe together and making sure that people can survive on this earth. Most of us are still practicing love. That is what we are all here for on Earth.

The love in our hearts is more than just a feeling. I remember what I read about in John Selby´s book *Let Love Find You* – that love is an actual condition in the muscular and hormonal tone in our hearts. There, he describes that the Princeton Engineering Anomaly Study, over 20 years, studied that our hearts and minds broadcast an energetic power outward into the environment that can demonstrably influence the performance of very sensitive electronic equipment.

The heart generates an electromagnetic field that radiates outward into the environment, just as our bodies as a whole radiate an energy field, and our planet likewise. The electromagnetic field of your heart broadcasts an energetic expression of how you´re feeling in your heart outward – and the field changes its configuration considerably depending on what emotion you´re feeling in your heart.

Furthermore, this broadcast's power does not diminish with distance.

Also, it was discovered that if examining people in a state of happiness or love, the results were not double but six times stronger than with individuals in a non-loving and non-joyful state. This means that love and happiness at scientific levels are not only inner feelings, but that they are demonstrable forces that reach out and affect the world. When we talk about the power of love, we're talking about real power. It is a force that each of us can choose to increase within our hearts and minds and souls, and broadcast outward.

The Princeton study concluded that no distinct boundary exists between mind and matter at the wave and particle level of reality. This means that really, we all are one, and whatever one person feels and thinks affects everything else, always.

I ask Singhi why I have experienced so many unusual events in Bhutan. He explains: »Because it is normal to believe in unseen things of the soul, they simply are easier to notice here than in the West. There are no distractions, it is the entire country's frequency and energy saturation here. It is part of our reality.«

I think of the memories from my childhood that are coming back, every day new ones. It is all starting to make sense.

4. Star Family

I am lying in bed, awake. The moon is shining brightly tonight. I am a little girl, 7 years. A second later, riding on what seems like a beam of the moon, something very bright zips into my room. Two figures, tall, with a bluish shimmer to them. They seem very familiar, I am not afraid. They don't talk, but I hear – in a different way - what they are saying.

»We are here so that you remember. Would you like to come with us and see where you are from?« I nod. A second later we ride up the moon's beam and are somewhere completely different.

It is very familiar to me. We are in some sort of area, space. It has multi-levels and is very high, almost like a dome, but I can't see the ceiling nor walls. I don't notice any boundaries. It appears endless. There are many more beings. It is not crowded but spacious. And relaxed. Inbetween there are what might be a different kind of plants – not like those I have seen at home but in different colors and with different textures.

There seem to be two types of beings: tall ones with a bluish shimmer and short ones, not much taller than I, with robes. »We are one family. It is just like on Ekarth: You have humans of many different skin colors – yet you are the same human family. The blood in all your veins is red, no matter what your skin color«, explains one of those accompanying me, as if reading my thoughts. »And yes, we talk telepathically.«

We are not walking but nonetheless moving forward in a kind of motion. Not floating; more like swimming, except we are not in water.

»Remember when you return back to Earth, to keep an open mind for this here«, says the other one accompanying me. »Tens of thousands of years ago, on Earth, if somebody in Europe would have said humans exist who are black, that person would have been considered crazy. Then it became a reality. Your technology developed so that you could travel – and you saw with your own eyes that there are black people, white, red, yellow. And now, as evolution again moves on, many of you already know that there are more beings than just you humans in the universe. Many of you remember because it is where you come from.«

My heart laughs inside, I feel happy and at home beyond words. I know this is true. How often have I felt so very strange with humans on Earth. Often I have wondered how strange my parents´ behavior was, also that of other adults. I just couldn´t make any sense of why people did and said some things.

I absorb as much as I can as we glide on. We pass pulsating areas and corners. The star beings seem to relax there, sitting and lying. Then there areas which are glowing white and yellow. The beings there are doing something, but not manually.

»We brought you here so that you remember. We can mark one of your fingers so that you know your visit here was real after you return. It won't hurt. Would you like that?« I think a moment, then nod. I would like to know this is really true, happening.

One of the fingers on my left hand pulsates, I look at it. There are two perfect small rings on it now, like the endless eight. Two circles entwined in each other:

There are several star beings here now, about a dozen, both the short and the tall ones. I feel so happy to see them, tears shoot into my eyes. »She remembers«, they say to each other. »Yes, you have known us all for a very very long time. We have come to see you.«

They surround me and I feel myself being charged with love and energy. I look at one star being, intently. »Yes, we too have known each other many times.« Instinctively I know it has something to do with a love relationship. My heart glows. I look at the other ones. With each one there is a different feeling – such as with friends, siblings, parents, beloved teachers. I feel happy.

It is time to return home. The same two who picked me up ride back down the moon's beam with me. A second later I am back in my room. And they are gone.

I look at my finger, turning on the light. There they are, two small rings:

∞

To this day, when I show my mother the marking on my finger, she doesn´t know where it came from. She cannot remember my being burnt or injured or having an infection. She most certainly would have noticed that somehow – by my crying or her washing my hands and seeing it. Instead, the two rings simply appeared. She was very surprised when I showed them to her in the morning.

Nowadays, my mother is open for the possibility that there is more to life than what the eyes can see. When we talk about such matters, she usually mentions that I used to be a sleepwalker when the moon was full. It is her explanation of why I see angels and other beings, even though she can´t explain what my having sleepwalked has to do with it when I ask her. Then she simply says that I often wandered around the house. She would wake up from the sounds I made and come up to me. I was not aware of her even though my eyes were wide open. I was in a trance.

My mother understands much more of these things than she will admit: sometimes she says things that are very clear. But she is cautious and will never openly talk about it, as I do, naming angels and star beings. She is still part of a generation in which such phenomena are not accepted socially as they are in Bhutan and other countries.

In her generation, the mystical was stigmatised. In the generations before her, people talking about such matters were even prosecuted, killed or locked up in mental asylums. Even though *The Bible* is full of tales about angels, to this day if a person openly says he talks with angels on a daily basis, he is considered insane or a liar.

Consequently, as a child, when I do tell my mother about my star family, angels or other unusual events in the invisible world, she explains I have a beautiful but vivid imagination. It isn´t real, she says. And so, slowly over the course of years, when I see other beings or go into a trance again, I dismiss it as imagination. By the time I am a teenager I am shut down to the other world.

It isn´t until many years later that I understand why sleepwalkers don´t notice they are carrying their body around with themself in their dream. Often they are seekers – looking for their spiritual home, for the reason of life, for themselves. They sense that there is more than everyday life. They search for this at night, with their astral body, and their physical body tries to come with them. When a sleepwalker awakens to his spiritual nature and lives his dreams in everyday life, arriving in himself, then he doesn´t have to search at night anymore and stops sleepwalking. I also did.

5. The Invisible World and Orbs

It is a great mystery why and that a world and universe exist around us. Creation is magical and mystical, and we are part of it. Nothing is as nourishing and satisfying as feeling embedded in and connected to life and the wonder of it all, trusting in its natural flow. Then, you find your own unique place in life. You realize you are part of the spirit world. All beings– whether human or spirit – have a spirit, are consciousness.

Many people in the West have a yearning for the mystical in their life; me too. Over the course of many years I study about the invisible world with different teachers all around the world. About how to enter and move around in it. How to connect with the juice of creation and bring this vital life energy back into everyday reality. How to have power in a good and balanced way. About different spirit beings and how to communicate with them and receive their help.

Being able to do all this is similar to a radio or TV tuning into different stations. Even though you can't see the frequencies of the stations, they are there. You just need a device, technology to tune into them.

Shamanic techniques and ceremonies are the technology which help me tune into the invisible world and communicate with its different entities. One of these techniques, found worldwide universally amongst indigenous cultures, is to go into a meditative or trance state. In this condition, your brainwaves change from an awake beta state to a calmer alpha into a deeply relaxed theta state – shifting from 30 to 4 hertz. Your are awake but very relaxed, in a different frequency. Thus, you too are able to receive different vibrations, much like the radio or TV that is tuned into different stations with different frequencies.

Many scientists and artists say their best ideas came to them in this kind of trance; they didn´t happen from the mind. Albert Einstein, when asked, said that he didn´t think of his theory of relativity – instead it appeared suddenly while he was dozing, like a vision. Not awake, not sleeping – but in a state of deep relaxation and trance with theta brainwaves. It is the state in which we are tuned into the natural flow of energy behind everything.

Albert Einstein was searching for a universal truth. He received an answer from the juice and energy flow of the universe.

Since digital cameras are on the market, there is a phenomena of bright, transluscent shapes appearing in photographs. Digital cameras are able to pick up more of the light spectrum than we can normally see with our naked eye. These phenomena appear in different forms. One most commonly seen in photographs are round glowing spheres of light called orbs. They are of different sizes, often with intricate designs and patterns.

These orbs are evidence of the other realms, of the invisble world. They are not merely photographic anomalies, dust or water drops – confirmed by Stanford physics professor and materials science researcher at NASA Klaus Heinemann in the documetary *Orbs – The Veil is Lifting*.

Such orbs appear behind objects, such as branches or chairs and clearly not close to the camera's lens. An orb can show detailed patterns that wouldn't be in focus if it was close to the lens. The same orb can appear in more than one photograph.

The invisible world is becoming visible with modern-day technology. Orbs are a scientific explanation of the lightballs I saw in Bhutan – except I experienced them without the aid of a camera, in a meditative and intuitive state.

There are also many historical references, tales and paintings that relate to the orb phenomenon, such as cherubs, angels, fairies, spirits and many others. Some modern day teachers of the ancient Eastern energy exercise of Chi Kung speak of the orbs as balls of energy that can communicate and help heal.

Orbs have been photographed around sacred sites and are appearing more and more. Orb-sites can be cultivated: The more pictures taken, the more the orbs appear. This implies that they have a consciousness. Also, they seem to react to people's emotions, appearing in greater numbers when people are feeling love, joy, bliss or meditating – and around children.

6. Shamanism

With the right techniques, everybody can learn to see and communicate with the invisible world – even without a digital camera. You also don´t have to be an Albert Einstein to receive divine inspiration.

Methods that do this are shamanic practices that have been passed on orally for 45.000 years and are considered the oldest healing forms in existence. They developed from the laws of nature and are performed by all indigenous cultures attempting to live in balance with nature. Whether Indian tribes in the Americas, African cultures such as the Dogan, Yoruba or Bushmen, the Australian Aborigines, Siberian and Mongolian indigenous people, Eskimos – they all share similar practices and rituals to heal and live in harmony with existence by connecting with the invisible world.

In shamanism, people are taught that communicating with the source of all, the divine, is a natural part of life. Indigenous cultures start early with initiation ceremonies for youngsters. The methods are simple and easy to understand, everybody can do them.

Common techniques are: a trance induced through drums or sounds, dance or certain postures. Communicating with power animals. Extracting or removing the source of an illness. Times of vision quest and rites of passage for all age groups. Working with ancestors. Soul retrieval work – bringing back parts of the soul which have left us.

These shamanic healing methods were officially accepted by the WHO – World Health Organization – in 1980 as equally effective in healing psychosomatic disturbances as is modern psychotherapy, as well as to stay healthy and balanced.

What is universal to all of these ways in which people connect with the invisible world: They cause deep transformative sensations in the body and soul. When you do these practices, things really do shift – you are not just thinking about them. They change and affect your biochemistry, hormones, digestive system, your cerebral spinal fluid. You are not just studying a philosophy with your mind, but living it with your entire being. The results are real and physical.

Shamanic practices are a pathway to freedom to find your life´s purpose and thereby love and health in the here and now. This is a path to yourself, with yourself, embedded in the world, nature and the universe, connected with everything. There is no guru or priest as the only bridge and communicator with God.

These methods teach how to recognize and feel the energy behind everything - the matrix, the invisible world - God. In this ancient philosophy, the visible, physical life is considered a reflection of the invisible world. If you are in balance in your soul and with the energy behind everything, you are in harmony and empowered in reality.

All matter is energy – that was Albert Einstein's breakthrough theory of relativity. The old shamans already knew and worked with this tens of thousands of years ago. Everything is pure light, in its smallest unit, moving at the speed of light. In shamanic healing work, you are able to work with this energy, this light – often traveling huge distances through the matrix and universe.

It only takes an instance for me to leave the Earth. I have entered some type of wormhole and am

zipping through tunnels. Suddenly, very quickly and abruptly, I am there. A strange place in a far away galaxy.

I see a bubble floating between stars. Inside is a small child-soul, alone. It left its physical body when it was four years. There was a lot of violence in its family, too much to bear. It had to go as far away in the universe as it could possibly get, to a distant galaxy.

Now, the physical body is almost 50 years. The man has come to me and asked to heal his broken childhood. I am working with him and in a trance. I ask his child-soul if it wants to come back, after 46 years. It is only too happy to and starts crying.

This happens without talking verbally. With my spirit guides I bring the child-soul back through the wormholes and help it reenter the man's body.

In that moment, tears come to the man's eyes and his entire body breathes out, relaxes.

7. New Shamanism

In my work, I have supported thousands of people to find their connection to the source again and trust it. These people come from all different backgrounds and professional areas. Like I once, they are looking to understand events from their lives encountering angels, star or spirit beings. They would like to be able to communicate with them.

When I ask the people I work with why they want this, there is a common thread: the feeling and wish that there is more to life than what we get taught and shown in the Western world. There is a longing for something higher, something noble with a purpose, the source or God; something full of integrity and love for all beings, mankind, and the universe.

They would also like to find out what their purpose is in all of this, here in this lifetime on this planet; something more meaningful than rushing around between the office, home and shopping. Their talent and unique gift to this planet.

When these people talk about this they are often insecure and ashamed, with awkward words trying to explain that which is so difficult to put into words. Often there is fear of being condemned or judged in some way – I can hear how their voices tremble.

This moves and touches me every time. It reminds me of when I start on my quest. I also feel very insecure and even have panic attacks I cannot place. Until, in a healing session with one of my teachers, I see why I am so afraid.

I look down at my feet. They are wrapped in shoes that I don't own and don't know in this lifetime. I am wearing a long, brown skirt. I am sitting in the forest; simply sitting, looking. Next to me is a basket full of leaves, roots and herbs. I know what to do with them.

I am looking at a beautiful, large, ancient tree. It is talking to me, telling me how I can help one particular woman with her illness.

I go to her house and give her my plant remedies. But as I do so, a man – her husband – runs up to me, shouting that this is devil's work. He starts hitting me. Other men and women from the town come and start beating me. I am kicked and stabbed to death by the mob. It is terrifying and gruesome.

It is a fact that in the Middle Ages an estimated 6-7 million people were killed during witch hunts over the course of several hundred years. No other culture has in such a short period of time succeeded in destroying its own natural connection to and knowledge of the divine as western civilization. The only remnants are legends of ancient shamanic healing in the nordic song collection of the *Edda* as well as in tales of the Celts in the British Isles. Everythings else was systematically wiped out.

Those killed were often women, but also men. Any person of knowledge was a threat to the church's claim for power that only priests were able to communicate with the divine. Certainly there were individual religious leaders full of integrity and respect for humanity within the church. But as a collective institution and being, it felt threatened by those who knew about healing with nature – as did every western country conquering indigenous nations worldwide at any point in history.

Any person able to communicate with animals and nature, heal with herbs, with knowledge of the stars; anybody who knew how to go into trance and talk with the spirit world and ancestors was condemned. Basically, anybody who lived with an open, free heart and mind was sentenced to death. And since shamanic techniques are passed on orally and through hands on learning, the only way to destroy them was to kill.

Many people have such memories – burnt on the stake, decapitated, hung, whipped, tortured, beat. Whether they are personal memories from past lives or collective memories of human history on this planet, I do not know. It doesn't really matter, because these memories and feelings are here, stored in our cells and cell memory passed on from generation to generation. These events really did happen.

There is a collective need to honor and heal them – only then can these awful events dissolve and be replaced by individual human dignity and freedom.

Whereas in Europe the methods were destroyed entirely, in other parts of the world – the indiginous Americas, Africa or Australia -, brave people were able to carry on the knowledge underground, even though it often meant risking their lives.

It is only since 1978, for example, that Native Americans and Hawaiians are allowed to practice their spiritual beliefs and techniques, so permitted by the Religious Freedom Act. Until then, you could and did go to prison – and in earlier years sentenced to death - for conducting a sweatlodge and other ceremonies, doing soul retrieval, Huna and shamanic healing work.

In finding our roots again, westerners have been first turning to the intact shamanic knowledge of these indigenous cultures. However, shamanic wisdom developed from universally applicable truth. It was learned over tens of thousands of years from trial and error and became common knowledge which helped people survive. Reopened to this universal and natural wisdom inherent in our cell memory, westerners too have found the connection again.

It is not without reason that so many young people in modern-day culture dance all night long to pounding beats. Without understanding it, they enter a trance and into transcendental experiences, a state of being closer to the source. In indigenous cultures, young people are prepared for adulthood in rites of passage by dancing in trance for hours. Also later, as adults, many ceremonies are performed with dancing in such a way, oftentimes ecstatically. The North American Indian Sun Dance is an example of this, in which entire tribes come together to this day to dance, sing and play drums, thereby entering a healing state of trance.

A new kind of shamanism has developed in western countries, with many different names such as hypnotherapy, matrix healing, quantum healing or reiki. There is a resurgence of something that was destroyed which can never be destroyed – because it is the healing essence of everything.

»Who knows«, my teacher tells me, »who we were before. Maybe you were an Indian shaman. And now I am helping you remember this knowledge so that you can be part of it rising in collective awareness again for the West. Maybe I once was a ›bad guy‹ during the Medieval Inquisition. And now am a Native American shaman with a real understanding - because of my gone astray past life. I realize how important it is to open our knowledge to westerners to rekindle what once was destroyed.

Nobody is completely good or completely bad. In our core, every soul, every heart is a shining and bright crystal light. In some people it is covered more and needs to be cleaned and polished. In others, it is already shining openly. But no matter what, we all carry the same crystal light inside.«

As I continue opening myself for universal knowledge and the invisible world, I pass through a past-life memory where I myself was a prosecutor, a »bad guy« once. I am shocked and disgusted; this is very difficult for me to come to terms with. But it is an invaluable process for me. Realizing that, I too, once, hurt others out of fear of the unknown, loss of control, greed and for power – and forgiving myself for it. This helps me develop compassion for those who today are harming others, astray on their path; understanding how the mechanism of the Beast in each one of us functions.

Everybody has already done wrong. This understanding helps me let go of judgement, of the polar and dual concept of good and bad. We are all here to learn and grow. Forgiveness is here for everybody – but you yourself have to decide to forgive yourself. We humans have free will; it is entirely up to us when we are ready to tackle and solve certain issues. The universe is endlessly patient.

When you are ready to let go and open yourself to the joy, beauty and lightness of life – the universe will provide this for you also.

8. Dolphins and Whales

My first encounter with dolphins is in Florida as a teenager. We are visiting my parents´ friends there. They have a small sailboat. One afternoon, as we are out in it, some dolphins suddenly show up out of the nowhere. I feel happy. You can´t help but love dolphins. They make everybody smile.

The dolphins stay with us for a while, swimming next to us. They are so near, I can hear their squeaks and whistles, their strong outbreath, the water spouting out of their breathholes. I see their eyes looking up at each one of us very intelligently, just like another human. That is what startles me the most. They are checking us out.

I could reach out and touch them with my hand. But I don´t, feeling it would be intrusive to do so; that I could only touch them if they did so first. I would love to jump in the water and swim with them like in the television-series *Flipper*, but never in the world do I think that I can actually do that.

Six years later, I am on my way home from my year-long backpacking trip around the world. My last stop are the Canary Islands off the northern coast of Africa. I will swim with dolphins for the first time there. I saw them several times in India and Thailand, even a humpback whale in Bali. Every time, I feel myself coming closer to them energetically as well as physically.

Then, I hear somebody say that it is actually possible to swim with them in the wild. I know I am ready. They have also been showing up in my dreams frequently: I am surrounded by one or several dolphins, swimming and gliding together. The dreams are always beautiful, loving. I wake up from them feeling fulfilled and happy.

By now I have learned about the universal law of attraction. That events will come your way if you invite them in and are open for them. Scientifically this phenomenon is described as resonance, which is the inherent capacity of different things or people to vibrate in harmony with and attract each other.

I will meet the right person to show me how to swim with the dolphins. I don't want to swim with captive dolphins – they should be free and come to me because they really want to.

It doesn't take long until I meet a woman in Thailand who tells me about a shamanic healer who takes people to swim with the dolphins. I know instinctively that she is the right one. She becomes an important teacher for me.

We leave shore that first morning in a small rubber dinghy with an outboard motor: Sali, her captain, a woman with her two sons and myself. Before we leave, Sali offers prayers to the sea, asking for permission for us to visit it and the dolphins in their home; in their living room. I am touched by the respectful way she does this. We sing a song – she says the dolphins love music.

Sali tells us that we shouldn't be disappointed if the dolphins don't come, that we shouldn't expect too much – you never know, after all, they are wild and free. We should just enjoy the moment. So I do just that. Though inside I feel they will come.

My intuition is right. Just half an hour later we meet a large group of dolphins, at least a hundred. They appear out of nowhere; suddenly they are here. This is a phenomenon particular to dolphins. Often it seems that they show up out of nothingness, materializing.

We are surrounded by beautiful dolphins; several pods coming together, explains Sali, they like to play together. And play they do! We watch them swim around each other in pirouettes, rubbing against each other. Jumping, splashing, chasing each other. My heart leaps with joy.

Sali tells us we can get ready to enter the water. Gently I slide into the ocean, trying not to splash loudly, the way Sali explained to us earlier. My heart is pounding, I look around through my mask. I see them! They are below me, beside, ahead of me. All over! So fluent, so multidimensional. I feel like I am with my star family again – suddenly there is a memory flash, a recognition.

One dolphin quickly swims up to me. If I didn't know they are gentle beings I would expect him to bang right into me. He zooms to a halt exactly infront of me. Just a little closer and he would touch me. I feel his energy field and sense it is a male because he is very large, one of the bigger ones I see. I see him looking into my eyes – like in Florida on the first dolphin encounter from the sailboat. A second later he swims away.

Sali had explained to us earlier that we should resist the temptation to swim after the dolphins. That would only chase them away. Instead, we should wait. They would return. Like the in- and outbreath, like waves moving in and out, like the rhythm in friendships and relationships of spending time together to being alone again to spending time

together again. The dolphins, too, have this rhythm.

The big dolphin turns, and indeed, comes back. Only to swim away again a few seconds later. I look around to see if there are other dolphins. I see the people from the boat in the water. Then, as quickly as they came, the dolphins disappear again, swimming into the deep, out of sight.

As we dry off on the boat, Sali tells us this was a very powerful encounter because there were so many dolphins. When so many come, she says, it is an initiation. Since each dolphin has its own sonar with frequencies comparable in strength to medicinal ultrasound, they literally penetrate us deep down into the core of our cells. This way, they open us up by activating our DNA structure. And the more dolphins, the stronger the field is.

Sali gives an offering of herbs to the sea, thanking mother ocean and the dolphins. We sing a song for the ocean.

We continue on our journey. I sit quietly, like the others, looking at the sea. None of us feel like talking – so precious was this experience. It echoes in my cells.

An hour or so later, we again see fins near our boat. But this time they are much larger. Pilot whales, Sali explains. These are very large dolphins, though many people think they are whales. This time it is a small group, maybe half a dozen of them. Their skin is dark grey. They have big and plump bodies, about the size of a large van. They are moving slowly.

Sali takes out some small bells and rings them near to the water. They seem to like this because they move very close to the boat.

Sali nods to us to get in the water again, but the woman shakes her head, her face is green. She looks like she is seasick. The teenage boys and I get ready. A minute later we are in the water.

The pilot whales are right next to us. Now I realize just how large they are. I don't feel nervous but I notice that the boys get on the boat again. I look at Sali and she nods that it is safe for me to stay in the water by myself. I trust these gentle giants.

I lay in the water looking through my mask and breathing through my snorkel, swimming forward very slowly. One pilot whale swims with me on my left, the other on my right. If I would stretch out my arms I could touch them; that's how close they are. But again, I feel that it would be intrusive to do so, and resist. They are so large, but instead of fearing their size I feel cushioned by them on either side, protected and safe.

Then, a third pilot whale shows up exactly under me, just a few feet down. I sense it is a female. She turns her belly towards me. I am in awe. Two pilot whales to the right and left, one below me belly up – I am in a total trance. We swim like this for quite a while, forming a kind of unit, the four of us.

I feel energy flowing into me, I sense an immense opening inside my body and cells. They are communicating with me. It is what I call downloading. Nonverbal, yet a large amount of information is being transported into me. It feels wonderful, very ancient and full of wisdom.

I start to shiver and realize I must have been in the water for a long time. Sali must sense it also, because I hear her voice muffled through the water. In the thrill of the moment, it is easy to become unaware of the body cooling down too much from the water. I swim back to the boat and climb up. I am shivering. I wrap myself into my towel and eat some fruit and nuts Sali shoves into my hands.

I look at the water; the whales are still there. They stay with us for another half hour or so, right next to our boat, as if they were calling me to come back in. But I am too cold, don't have a wet suit yet. I watch the pilot whales from the boat, feel their energy.

»They really like you«, Sali says to me. »This is very special.« I also sense the specialness of this occasion. It is the kind of event that only happens a few times in a lifetime. If you recognize it and don't rationalize or downplay it, it shifts your entire reality and way of looking at life about who you authentically are; what your life purpose is and what you came to do on this planet in this lifetime.

I now know exactly that my life will always be connected to the whales and dolphins. This is the recognition of something I have sensed often before but not quite believed yet because it is so awesome and beautiful. The dolphins and whales are part of my family. »Yes, it is true«, I feel them saying, »you are linked with us, you have work to do with us. We will help heal you, and you will help others heal through us.«

Time has gone by quickly, it is time to return back to our home base on shore. We sing our farewell to the whales and thank them. They disappear, understanding our message.

A few minutes after they are gone the woman on the boat starts vomiting, even though it is a calm sea. Spasms shake her whole body, even after there is nothing more in her stomache to come out. I sense that it has something to do with the whales. Later, Sali confirms this as I ask her. »Yes, their frequencies penetrate our tissues and cells very deeply and rinse out everything in this way. Opening and cleansing.« This particular woman had just gone through a divorce from her sons´ father. She needed to vomit out all the pain and sadness and anger and other emotions from the separation. Purge and cleanse and let go.

Over the years that I am allowed to work with the whales and dolphins, I often observe this: that people come to open their heart because the dolphins and whales have this healing quality. With the opening of the heart all suppressed feelings rise up which block the heart to be what it is: open and vibrating love energy. I too often cry when I swim with the whales and dolphins. It is the kind of crying that just feels wonderful. Your heart, your whole soul comes back to life, full of love.

I am grateful for being allowed to work with the whales and dolphins. I purposefully call it »being allowed«, because it is their choice also. They are living beings, possibly far more intelligent than we humans. I consider it an honor. The same applies to my work with the angels and spirit guides: I am grateful for »being allowed« to do this.

That evening, I dream of the pilot whales. They are outside the window in the bay, singing their song. They are calling my name, telling me they are so happy that I have come. I dream of them on and off all night. Inbetween I wake up, lying in bed hearing the waves lapping onto shore outside.

The next morning, Sali tells me that the dolphins and whales were in the bay all night.

I have come home to my family.

9. Spirit-Lines

I have memories of being a dolphin in a past life. It is a deep knowing as well as feeling. When I am with dolphins I understand how they work. They sense this too. We communicate on a noverbal level. Much like with my star family. I feel at home with them.

What is family? It is more than just your lineage in this lifetime - your mother, father, grandparents, greatgrandparents, and so forth. Family also consists of your ancestors from previous incarnations.

Shamanism describes such ancestries as spirit-lines. With them, you awaken to a much broader circle of love and support than with just your relatives. They strengthen you because many people feel like strangers with their own blood parents and family.

In those past lives you sometimes were human, but not always. As humans, some people feel a strong affinity for a certain country, culture or region. It is as if they knew a certain area – because indeed they lived there once. It is part of their ancestry.

As non-humans, some people have old ancestry lines to the angels; they were an angel once. Or fairies, or mermaids and –men. Magical people, old shamans, star beings. I know a person who once was a lion and several people who were whales before. Even stones.

We are related to everything and everyone; in shamanism, everything is considered your ancestors and relatives. Some are more familiar, some less.

I realize that I once was also rock as I receive a powerful teaching from a natural stone wall in the forest. I am on a hike and pondering over a question in my life: Whether I have the skill and strength to not only walk a spiritual path, but also to work in it. I want to support people heal and connect with their soul and life´s purpose.

At this point, I have recently returned from my second backpacking trip around the world. My first trip – which starts in Bhutan and takes me over Nepal to India, Thailand, Bali and the Canary Islands -, lasts a year. Returning home from it, I soon find a job again with another magazine, this time for *Elle*. Only to quit 9 months later and embark on another 1,5 years of travel and study with various teachers around the world.

This second time, after I return, I am again working as a journalist, freelancing for various magazines. It is going well, articles about lifestyle and travel, interviews with personalities. And it gives me the time and space to continue studying and learning about the things I am interested in:

metaphysical matters about life and the universe, the soul and psyche.

Nonetheless I know I want to change my profession, that I would like to work in the spiritual area I have been studying. But I have absolutely no clue how to go about this.

As I ponder how I will do this, I rest and look at the beautiful rock wall which rises up majestically in front of me. Its shades of beige, yellow, red and grey are dabbed with a bit of green here and there from little plants miraculously growing out of the stone. There is a small and dark cave which looks like an animal lives inside it. Swallows, which built their nests in other small caves at the top of the stone wall, are flying back and forth acrobatically.

As I sit watching all this beauty, the rock speaks. The voice is ancient, old and deep. »Be patient, it is not time yet. Be assured, it will come. Then you will know what to do and everything will flow easily. The universe always supports what is in line with its energy.«

I wait for more. By now, 5 years after my first opening in Namibia with the Bushman spirit, it is normal to me that not only humans speak – but also spirits, entities, animals, plants. And now apparently also rocks.

»You know patience, you too have been one of us. Sitting patiently for aeons, watching everything move around you, absorbing, learning. Giving solidity, being like bone. This is what you too must do now.«

I smile, it feels right. It is true – it is not time to make radical life changes yet. I am doing well as a journalist, am professional at it. Better continue to learn, study in the spiritual realms. Quietly observe, absorb.

I remember what it was like to be a rock. This makes me feel very strong, and sets time and patience into a different perspective.

Powerful beings live in crystals and stones; souls which are full of love and surrender. Rock is dense and bundled energy in physical manifestation. It absorbs and stores cosmic lifeforce energy and light, dispensing and radiating it over the entire Earth. Crystals and stones are very important for the Earth to be healthy and strong. They also can help people become healthy again, both physically and emotionally.

The old cultures knew about the strength in rocks. The Celts built Stonehenge and other sacred sites with stones. Sacred sites using rock as building material can be found everywhere around the world.

Ancient Atlantians specifically worked with the strength of crystals. Their energetic constructions can still be found in the area of the so-called Bermuda Triangle in the Atlantic Ocean.

I have traveled to the Carribean to visit the dolphins. It is early morning and I am sitting on a catamaran. We are moving parallel to shore. I enjoy the breeze, the warm air, the turquoise crystal clear water. I close my eyes. To my surprise, I immediately see a transluscent pyramid. It is very large. I look at it closely and see that it is made out of crystals at its corners. I also hear sounds, like a singing of voices, but not earthly voices.

»Dolphins, there!« I hear somebody calling and open my eyes. Ahead of us dolphins are splashing. As we move closer, I see it is a small group, six of them with a baby. They are curious about our boat

and come near to look. But when we enter the water, they disappear.

I forget about the crystal pyramid the rest of day as we sail along the island's coast. We don't see any more dolphins that day, so I enjoy snorkeling the reefs. It is a beautiful, relaxing first day. Upon returning to shore, I eat a large and delicious, spicy Carribean meal and go to bed early.

That night, I dream. I am with a group of people, we are discussing something. They accompany me into a room, where I am given two rods. They look like they are each made entirely out of whole blue sapphires.

I sit down cross-legged on the floor, holding one crystal rod in each hand. I close my eyes and see the others sitting in other rooms, the same way, each also holding crystal rods in different colors – emerald green, ruby red, diamond clear.

We are communicating telepathically. Then, one of the people in our group gives a signal and we all hold the rods above our heads, crossed and concentrating on joining the energy of all our crystal rods together. As I do this, I feel an incredibly strong surge of energy flowing from the universe through the rods and through my body. It is warm and and intensely beautiful and radiating.

I wake up.

The next day, I decide to tell the captain about my dream that night as well as my vision with the pyramid the previous morning. I know he works *with energy himself and trust him. We are on our way out on his boat again, to visit the dolphins.*

»Honey«, he says to me in his southern US drawl, »we are right on top of the Road to Atlantis here. There are blocks right below our boat that have been dated 25.000 years old by scientists. They´re what´s left of Atlantis. And the crystal light pyramids - I´ve seen them too. Many have.«

Later that day, we snorkel over the Road of Atlantis and I see the huge slabs of rock still visible through their covering of algae and coral. I realize my dream that night was really a memory of a lifetime in Atlantis. We were, indeed, constructing energy fields with crystals.

When I facilitate seminars about family and ancestors, I also always include ancestry lines from previous incarnations. For this, we create categories such as angels, star beings, animals, wizards, shamans and so forth. Each category receives a specific place in the room with an object to mark that space. Then, the participants walk from one position to the next, like going from one radio station to the next. That way they can see if they tune in with any of those positions.

Interesting is that there is always a fairly even balance of people on each position. The universe knows how to balance itself. It confirms my deep understanding that the universe meant there to be multitude, variety. We are supposed to be different.

There is the source – the center of it all. However, this center is no actual geographic location. Instead, it is inherent in everything in the universe in each atom, person, being, entity; each plant and mineral. Everything is a spark from this source. And even though we are all different, we are indeed of one.

In my workshops, everyone finds a place. Some walk back and forth between two positions, finally deciding where they feel the strongest and most familiar connection. Then I ask the participants to share their experiences, feelings and memories. Many have tears in their eyes or cry while talking, so deep is their sense of feeling at home or of memories resurfacing again.

In one particular workshop, a man is on the position of the star beings. He hasn't spoken yet, standing silently, with tears running down his cheeks. He came to the workshop to support his wife come into balance with her parents and ancestry in this lifetime. I ask him why he is crying. »I just realized«, he says, as the tears continue to flow, »that I haven't been on Earth often yet. I think it's my first time.«

We sense his sadness of feeling foreign here; experiencing how strange and harsh life is on Earth compared to his old home in the stars. We stand silently, giving him space to release and remember.

After he cries, his eyes glow with new vigor and energy. He tells the group that he knows he has »work to do here for the good of the planet. I am supposed to be here, now I remember why.« Later, his wife tells me that she has rarely seen her husband cry, and never before so long and deeply.

Finding the connection to one's past ancestry is often moving, touching and empowering. It opens the connection to your old knowledge. Opening that door is like turning on a switch. You know these things, you have already learned them, you don't need to start all over again – you just need to remember and activate them. Your soul remembers.

In addition, you are connected to an ancient lineage. This gives you a great line of support behind you, strengthening your back.

I have this kind of experience while I am training for sweatlodge ceremonies. A sweatlodge is a healing and praying ceremony in nature using heat to cleanse. From the beginning, it is all so familiar and easy for me to learn and understand. I have done this before. Now, again in this lifetime, I am intitiated by my teachers and granted permission to conduct ceremonies.

Since then, whenever I sit in the sweatlodge, talking prayers and pouring water on hot rocks and burning herbs, it is as if a higher energy is flowing and talking through me. Sometimes I am astonished at the words of wisdom coming out of my mouth. I certainly don't always think of them, but there they are, coherent and healing. It is because I am directly connected to an ancient lineage of natural wisdom and to those who walked this path before me; to tens of thousand years of knowledge, tradition passed on from generation to generation.

10. Ancestors – Seven Generations

Many indigenous cultures have the concept of seven generations. Your ancestors´ actions up until the seventh generation before you have an affect on your life – both positive and negative. Contemporary scientific cellular research backs this ancient knowledge. Information, whether behavioral, emotional or physical, is stored in our cell memory and passed on in our DNA structure.

Our responsibility for the seventh generation means taking responsibility for our actions now. The deeds of every person continue to have an effect for a very long time. Before you make any important decision in any area of your life – ask yourself what the consequences will be for the seventh generation of your descendants. You have to be aware of what kind of world you are leaving for them.

Ask the future to appear before your inner eye and see if the people will do well from your decision or not. Don´t create unncessary suffering.

This means cleaning up your footsteps, which is another wonderful concept I learned from old shamanic wisdom. Every step you take – do it in consideration of the ground you are treading on. Even though Earth is strong and a wonderful transformer – she can take much negative and transform and release it into new, positive – still there is a limit.

Whatever you put anywhere, pick it up and put it away yourself. Not only physically, also emotionally. It means taking care of your emotional garbage, being responsible for that. Don't dump it on your children, grandchildren or further generations.

Equally, what was not taken care of by the generations before you can weigh down on you. There are shamanic techniques such as the Hawaiian *ho'oponopono* or African work with ancestor lineages to release these and bring healing. I do this kind of clearing work in my family and ancestor courses as well as in individual sessions.

These ancient techniques too are backed by modern scientific cellular research in the area of genetic diseases. This shows that cells can be influenced by the environment and that negative information can be removed.

Ancestors are central and vital for every indigenous culture. There is the awareness that when family members pass, they are not simply gone. Life doesn't simply stop when you die. Each ancestor still affects the entire clan. If everything is in balance in a good way and we honor our ancestors, then the strength gained from the family line backing you is immense, the potential in your genes can fully unfold.

Those who came before me – I honor you – you have paved the way for me. This understanding gives you more power for your life. That is why so much importance is placed on clan lines and names, clan stories and myths.

Coming to peace with parents and ancestors is one of the biggest challenges and learning grounds for most people. But without our parents, none of us would be alive – regardless of how loving or not they are to us. Their gift to us is life. If we receive anything more from them, it is a bonus.

In looking for the connection to our parents, what we are really seeking is the connection to the source. Mother and father are, in essence, representatives for those forces, male and female principles, yin and yang, which let life reproduce, flourish and exist on our planet Earth.

This understanding helps take away the high expectations and demands we sometimes place on our mother and father – that they should be the source of all wisdom, strength and love. We realize that our parents and ancestors are not the source, not god - but only people doing the best they are able to, like everybody on this planet.

In honoring them in this way, they become an important gateway for us to the the great mystery of life. And we seek the source of everything because it is our ultimate home – where we come from when we are born and where we will return to when we die.

11. Death and Rebirth

My heart is racing. I feel myself collapsing inside – my circulatory, my respiratory systems. »Please god – don't take me yet. I am sorry.«

I have been rough on my body the last two months in India, driving it. Ignoring its signs of needing rest, despite being ill. Constant diarrhea, losing too much weight. Even losing my hearing for a while from dehydration. But I still cannot stop. I am driven, frantic.

I don't stop anywhere for long, I need to move on. I travel around the entire subcontinent, never staying anywhere more than a few days. Endless hours in buses and trains, countless temples, landscapes, villages, cities, faces, colors, smells pass by me. I never really arrive in India on my first trip there.

I travel on to Thailand. I want to attend a meditation retreat in a Buddhist monastery, learn how to meditate and calm my mind. Instead of taking the taxi, I decide to walk with my heavy backpack, after traveling overnight from Bangkok on the train. I think this will help calm my restlessness.

It is noontime, blazing heat. I am not wearing a

hat. I start to feel very dizzy and barely make it to check into a room in a guest house on the roadside. I set down my backback, go to the balcony in the back of my room to look out – and collapse.

My heart is too fast. I am lying on my back, staring at the sky. It is no longer blue, but suddenly very bright, a very intense light. The strongest light I have ever seen.

I know instantly that it is not from our earthly dimension; I know it is the light to the other world.

I whimper, realizing how serious my situation really is. I am alone, nobody is here to help me. My waterbottle is in the room, but I cannot move from the balcony to get it. The balconies next to mine are empty and I am to weak to raise my voice to call for help. I stare at the light and feel myself – parts of my essence - being sucked towards it.

I know instinctively that the tunnel to the other world starts behind it, even though I can't see it. I don't want to go there.

»I promise I will look after myself from now on,« I plead to God. There is no answer. There are no angels, nothing. I am alone with the light. It is so powerful. I have never experienced anything like it. It is beautiful in its magnificence – but I am terrified by it. I am not ready to go yet; I am too young.

I feel myself moving towards it – then back again. Then towards it again – and back, like a yoyo. I have to conjure all my willpower to stay here. I know if I let myself pass out now, I would be gone. That would be it.

I realize how much I value my life. How precious it is, how beautiful and wonderful. It is the first time I feel this. I see the inescapability of death; I see that life is about living it fully.

When we are young we think we will live eternally. Everybody at some point in their lives understands this is not the case, awakening to the realization that our existence in this lifetime is finite.

My struggle goes on all afternoon. I see the blazing light, the entrance to the other world above me. I move toward it, at one point seeing myself lying on the balcony from above; and I move back again.

Hours later, the bright light finally fades and the blue sky returns. I know I am back. I manage to crawl into the room and drink from my waterbottle. I find electrolytes in my backpack and drink them. I fall asleep.

The next morning I take a taxi to the next hospital. The examinations show that I have dehydration from the constant, two-month continual and untreated diarrhea from amoebas in my intestines – the cause of my diarrhea. I have a sun stroke from the long hike yesterday. And to top things off: dengue fever – a malaria-like fever transmitted my mosquitos.

»You are lucky«, says the friendly doctor. »Usually none of these alone are fatal – but together in this combination really can be.« I look at him. »You mean I could have died yesterday?«

He nods. »You have a good guardian angel that

made sure you are still alive.«

They keep me in the hospital on a drip for a few days, until the dengue subsides and I have put on some weight again. Then, the doctor urges me not to do a meditation retreat yet – but instead go to one of the nearby islands to a nice resort to rest and eat for a few weeks.

I follow his advice. I know that this is a wakeup call – and another opening - for me.

12. Regressions –
Past Life Memories

My bungalow directly on the beach is beautiful, with a little veranda facing the ocean. The food in the resort is delicious, the people gentle, polite and friendly. I slowly come back to life. A British woman offers yoga in a sheltered area on the beach, so I occasionally go there too.

I sleep well, enjoy swimming in the ocean and walking on the beach. I read books and hang out with other travelers.

I ask myself how I let myself be so driven as to not notice earlier how ill I was. Usually I feel the signs of my body and live healthily, eat balanced and exercise regularly. I have no idea. I could have died. And: I saw the entrance to the other side – it really was a close call.

One evening, sitting together with the British yoga teacher and some of her other students over dinner, talking about how good the food is, I tell her about how ill I was before I came here. Dana nods and says she saw me when I came. »You looked like you saw a ghost.«

Her observation was exactly right and so I tell her

what happened, that I was so driven in India. Before that, in Bhutan and Nepal it was the exact opposite, I relaxed. But for some reason in India, everything started going downhill for me.

She says she could do a trance session with me to find out the cause of the illness. In it, I would be in deep relaxation. Then, my inner voice and knowing might provide the answer.

I trust Dana and feel like this might help me; worth a try. So a few days later, in her bungalow, I settle down on a mat as she asks me to listen to the waves gently lapping against the beach outside. She says I should ask my soul why I became so ill that I nearly died. Dana counts backwards and I start to feel very light.

I feel myself running, just running. Looking down at my feet, I see they are barefoot. I am a teenager, my heart is throbbing. I am unhappy. My heart is aching

»Why are you unhappy?«, asks Dana.

Immediately I know why. »Because I cannot be with the girl I love. She is from a higher caste than I am.«

I see her face. It is beautiful. We have known each other since our childhood. My parents work on her family's estate. It is in India.

»What happens then?« I hear my Yoga teacher's voice.

I see myself being driven off her family's land, chased away as a teenager. Everybody there knows how much the girl and I love one other. That is why I am being chased away. That is why I am running.

I end up in another city, manage to make a new living there, even eventually get married and have children. But I never forget my childhood love; I never get over her.

Many years later, I return to the estate to visit my parents – they are still living there and old by now. But she is gone, herself married somewhere else, to somebody appropriate from her caste.

I hear my yoga teacher's voice like from a distant planet. »What does this have to do with your falling ill and almost dying?«

I remember feeling driven, frantic, never being able to stop. »I never healed that wound of not being able to be with her,« I answer. »Of being driven away.«

Suddenly, it becomes crystal clear: Traveling in India brought up those old memories in my soul, the old pain and immense grief that never healed. »I never had a chance to say goodbye to her«, I say. Tears run down my cheeks, I am surprised at the intensity of my emotions. »We played together as children and promised to marry each other one day.« I cry for a long time; tears that I didn't cry then, in that past lifetime.

When no more tears come, my yoga teacher gently talks: »You can say goodby to her now.« She asks me to call my childhood love and I see her face appear. Now, I see how sad she was too about my being chased away, in shock. I see how glad she is to see me. We hug each other for a long, long time. Our embrace is healing, allowing the love to flow and circulate that was forbidden then.

I feel the deep and intense pain again. Deep love, not able to be lived, experienced, fulfilled – it is one of the biggest pains there is. »That is why I couldn't stop in India, why I was so frantic; because the pain was too much to feel. So I kept on running and didn't even notice when I started falling seriously ill.«

Now, with the help of my yoga teacher, I am able to finally find peace that I was not able to live that love with my childhood sweetheart.

In the days after the regression, I feel this old pain I often had in my heart – but never knew why – slowly receding. I light a candle and do a ceremony to let this past experience finally pass by, finding peace with it. Letting it go, so that I may live and love fully now, in this lifetime.

That, for me, is the essence of why I do regression work. It helps make peace with the past, no matter what happened. Accept it as it is, forgive others and yourself.

In regression work, both the healer and the client enter the matrix, the invisible world, to work there. The client´s memories and the healer´s visions of past lives may be true or not, may be actual memories or just pictoral translations of collective events we as human individuals have tapped into. It doesn´t matter. The work in regressions affects the entire body of the client, biochemistry, brain and energetic structure to change for the better; that is what counts.

The movie *The Matrix* tapped into the ancient wisdom of shamanic healing – in it, too, the protagonists travel into the matrix to change the course of events in past, present and future. Time and space do not exist. Some regressions even go into the future, to help transform destructive patterns. The potential for everything is always here.

I stay in the resort a few more weeks and then travel to the monastery to do the Buddhist meditation retreat. It is two weeks and in silence, learning about Buddhism, with endless hours of sitting and walking meditation.

There, with the techniques I am taught, I let my thoughts pass by, like clouds. I slowly exit the windmills of the mind and enter a new type of being, presence. Sitting, observing – regardless if what I am observing is pleasant or not – not immediately reacting. Being.

I have time to reflect on what happened these last few weeks and months. I don't know if it is true that I had this past life in India – even if it feels very real. I wonder if I tapped into some type of collective memory there. But even if that is the case, it shows that everything indeed is connected.

One of our teachers, a Thai Buddhist monk, talks about the cylce of life, death and rebirth we repeat so long, until we are enlightened. For him and in Buddhism, past lives are a normal concept.

During our silent retreat, we are allowed interviews so I decide to meet this particular monk to tell him about my experience and ask him what he thinks about it. It is a short conversation – purposefully kept to the point as to not distract from the process of silence.

I tell him about my regression into a past life and ask him if it really could be true. His answer is crystal clear: »Yes, by all means. But it is not now, it is not important. Let go of the story, let go of your attachment to this girl; this is what causes the suffering. Everything passes by. There is only the present, which in a moment is a new moment. That is happiness.«

I am delighted with his answer and even more delighted that I actually understand it. But I have other questions now: If there really is reincarnation, where do we come from when we are born? Where do we go when we die and what are we then? How does this birth and rebirth thing actually work?

13. Bardo Thodol – the Tibetan Book of the Dead

Several religions and a third of the people on this planet officially believe in reincarnation. This does not automatically mean that an afterlife exists. This concept may be an escape from a miserable reality. But there is the possibility.

Many people in the West are sceptical of some sort of continuation of existence after dying. Either they don´t believe in it or think it´s absolute nonsense because there is no proof. The latter is true and also not.

There are numerous scientific reports and books of clinically dead people on the operating table or in accidents who came back to life and can tell about the experience. However, reanimated people only go a small path of what is there after dying because they return into the body again. They can describe the experience after clinical death - but not the entire detachment of the ethereal body, or the soul-consciosness from the physis. This raises the question if a soul separate from the body actually exists – or if when the body dies, our consciousness and soul die too.

People who have had an experience of clinical death and were reanimated nearly all speak about an intense light. They describe it as a blinding and bright light with an indescribable radiance.

When I first read such reports not long after completing my first Buddhist meditation retreat, I realize it is the same kind of light I saw in my near death experience. What is different, though, in my experience from those who were clinically dead, is that they were in the light – whereas I saw it from a distance and felt parts of myself being drawn towards it.

Next, I read translations and interpretations of the Bardo Thodol or the Tibetan Book of the Dead. This ancient Tibetan wisdom book is about death, the process of dying, afterlife and rebirth. It is considered the most detailed study and book of any culture about these topics. Whereas Western culture fears and avoids reflection about the inevitability of death, Tibetan culture does the opposite: embracing it as a means to a more happy and fulfilled life, in the light of the inevitable - dying.

The Bardo Thodol is not thought or made up but instead provides insights into death gained from observing natural laws. Tibet has a dry and cold climate in which the corpse decays slowly, which thus could be studied in detail, minutely. Tibetan monks and healers studied not only the body, but also the breath of the dying person, combining it with their ancient knowledge of using breathing to direct types and levels of consciousness and awareness during meditation. In this way, they wrote about the signs and levels of death and the detachment of the soul-consciousness from the physis based on both the body and the breath of the dying person in great detail.

Further, the authors of the Bardo Thodol combined their culture´s knowledge about life and the universe, meditation, spiritual awakening and enlightenment with dying.

Tibetan Buddhism never rejected its shamanic nature wisdom like the Western church did, proclaiming it devil´s work, but instead integrated the old knowledge. In its belief system, everything has a spirit-nature – every person, tree, stone, animal, planet, star. You are a soul who is making a human experience. The human part of you is a part of your being, but not your entire being.

For Tibetans, the essence of spirit is light, which is depicted repeatedly in their art. They knew all along what Albert Einstein discovered in the twentieth century: That all matter equals energy, and that energy in its smallest known particle is light. Solidity does not exist, because everything, in its tiniest part, is vibrating energy, vibrating light. This light and energy never disappears. Nothing gets lost in the universe, nothing goes to waste.

The ultimate spirit-nature of all things can also be experienced by achieving spiritual awareness during lifetime, according to Tibetan Buddhism.

Interesting is that the spiritual experiences of enlightenment in all cultures are described as a spontaneously appearing, unearthly light, like that described in near death or clinical death experiences.

From all this the Tibetans concluded that during the process of dying, the soul-consciousness of a person separates from the body. This usually doesn't happen abruptly except in sudden accidents and deaths. Instead, the separation occurs gradually over the course of days and weeks, which they also describe in great detail in the Bardo Thodol. The ethereal body moves away from the body, then gets pulled back like a yoyo, then moves away again.

This describes the exact process I go through that particular afternoon when I feel myself moving towards the light, then coming back again, then moving towards it again – over and over.

I have to say, because the phenomena I experienced are all described accurately in the Bardo Thodol, I now consider that there really is the possibility of some sort of continuation after death. Even if it may be far from anything we can ever imagine.

I am a sceptic and believe in what Buddha taught: »Don't believe what I say, find out through your own experience.« But I would like to enter the process of dying, when it is time, at peace and with as clear and conscious a mind and awareness as is possible, to then experience the biggest adventure of life - dying. If it turns out there is no continuation of some sort of existence of soul-consciousness, then it doesn't matter anyhow. I also take this possilbity into account. But if there is a continuation – then I am prepared.

There must be an unspeakable grandness and graciousness in dying peacefully, consciously, with complete awareness and in thanks of the life lived fully – including all experiences, embracing all that happened.

The Bardo Thodol also recommends an experienced, living guide for the dying and then dead person. Because in the Buddhist worldview everything is connected and it is possible to communicate with all realms, this loving and compassionate guide literally coaches the just dead person through the other realm, onto the right path, so that he won't get lost or astray as confused spirits sometimes do. This guiding of the deceased's spirit-soul is practiced to this day by Tibetan people.

I would also like to do it like this.

The Bardo Thodol explains that once the body has died, the soul-consciousness departs from it. Then it is in an intermediate state, which is the meaning of the word *bardo*, until it gains enlightenment or reincarnates.

There are several types of *bardos*. Some are frightening and confusing, bringing up unresolved issues from the person's last life. That is why it is good to have a guide to act as a coach to make it through the bardos well.

The Bardo Thodol describes that it takes about 13 days to overcome this intermediate state. However it is unclear whether this is an exact number or if it is meant symbolically that the deceased person's spirit-soul needs guidance the most in the first two weeks after his death.

There are a few remnants of the 13 days in our culture. The »wake by the body« was a similar tradition, sitting by the corpse for several days to weeks, accompanied with prayers for the deceased's soul. This practice has stopped though because nowadays it is considered unhygienic and not permitted for a dead body to stay outside that long.

This in my view is a reflection of the frantic fear in the West to look death in the eye, instead simply pushing it out of sight. Death is considered a general cut with which everything stops. Logically, we build a huge fear of dying which is the biggest block of fear humans can produce of anything.

But even if the dead bodies in the West are not permitted to remain outside long enough to sit by, it is still possible to do the wake by the body without the physical body present. The spirit-consciousness has departed from it and time and space do not exist in the invisible world.

If the fear of death fades, so the Tibetan teachings, the path is open for transformation. The more consciously we accept this process, the easier we are able to see a new perspective, a new possibility of being. And the easier we can let go of the body and allow the transformative process of dying.

The spirit-consciousness then goes on its pilgrimage in the light plane to achieve total liberation. It is the phase between the clinical death and the enlightenment of the deceased.

Not everybody achieves this, according to the Bardo Thodol. But everybody has the chance. Some may return into another incarnation to make further experiences. Some may continue to achieve experiences on different planets, stars and planes we do not know about. And some achieve enlightenment, returning to the source of all.

Interesting is that the word »death« isn´t used at all in the title of the Bardo Thodol. The focus of the book is about becoming free from the illusions of our limited and egocentric consciousness which separate us from the whole, from the source, from enlightenment.

14. Quantum Physics on Rebirth

So what is this spirit-consciousness, and where does it go? As so often, contemporary science is finding what ancient knowledge has known all along. Modern quantum physics and a number of serious physicists such as Amit Goswami, Pim van Lommel and Markulf H. Niemz back what is written in the Bardo Thodol with their findings.

Quantum physics studies the interactions of energy and matter and is a branch of physics. They believe that consciousness – that which we call the soul - is also a quantum-phenomenon like many others and call it »quantum consciousness«. According to quantum physics, such a consciousness does not necessarily need a physical carrier such as a living brain or a body. As a wave, consciousness can continue independently from a body.

They assume that consciousness is a quantum-physical field of information which can be received from the brain like electromagnetic waves are received from a television. It is assumed that this soul-consciousness has similarities with light – both are particles without mass but with quantumphysical qualities which exist without a doubt. They can influence each other over great distances. In this way, all souls are connected to one big whole – to the original state of light.

Quantum physics explains soul-consciousness as a process of consciousness that doesn't disappear with the detachment from the body – but goes into another phase of energy and matter. Which is exactly what the Bardo Thodol describes.

However, such a consciousness continuing onwards is impossible for us to imagine. Our emotions, thinking and actions need our body. Maybe that which remains is some type of flow of information, the experience of having had a body.

»Nothing is permanent. Everything is always changing – that is the only permanence in life,« I learned from the Buddhist monks at the retreat in Thailand. One of the main teachings in Buddhism is that everything passes. From this awareness is meant to come less fear of the unknown, of change, of death, less attachment – and more awareness in the now. And thus, happiness.

15. Medicine Wheel and the Purpose of Life

Shamanism too talks about constant change, describing it as a circle, neverending and with no beginning, represented in a medicine wheel. This is a circle usually made with stones, but also painted. It is a symbol of the universe, showing the connection of all life: elements, plants, animals, minerals, humans, spirit-world, planets and stars.

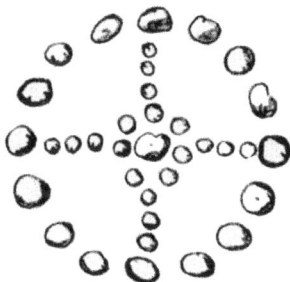

Medicine wheels can be found everywhere in the world. The more famous ones are from the Druids in Stonehenge, from the Mayas and other Native Indians of the North and South Americas. In India and Asia they can be found in the shape of mandalas.

Medicine wheels are places where people come together to celebrate life and for ceremonies, to heal and to learn about their place in life. They are holy, a home for the spirit world – a piece of the universe and sky on Earth, a gateway into the invisible world and a mirror of one´s position in it. They are a map of life where we can orient ourselves where we stand at any given moment, where we want to go and what the next necessary steps are.

You will always find yourself at changing positions in the medicine wheel, making different experiences in your life. But if you reflect, at any given moment, on what you can learn, then you can find balance in your life. Then there is stability, even if everything is constantly changing and even spinning around you.

Medicine wheels help heal blocks on all levels of being. The fear of dying may decrease or go away by realizing that everything is constantly changing. Your life purpose can become clear in working and feeling inside a medicine wheel.

Life purposes can be very different from person to person. For some, it is to experience and live love or to bring happiness and joy to those around them. For others, it is to help heal or to live fully a certain talent and gift, such as painting, singing, music, writing. And for some it is to live a simple and quiet life.

To be aware of what you want to be able to look back on when you leave this life is empowering and gives you a clear direction. The beautiful moments are what are fulfilling for our being. The Yaqui Indians have a precise way of bringing it to the point, when faced with decisions: »What shall I do now, knowing that I will die anyhow?«

For me, one of my purposes in this lifetime is to travel and simply enjoy this wonderful planet Earth.

16. Traveling

Humid and hot Brazilian jungle air. I am deep in the Amazon jungle. I have traveled here to see the pink river dolphin – the boto. It is considered very shy. So before I fly to Brazil, I already tell it telepathically that I am coming to visit – as I always do when I travel to visit the whales and dolphins. And would it please show itself.

It does – a lot - and isn't shy with me. I stay in the jungle for three weeks and it appears nearly every day.

The boto has a magnificent large body – and it really is very pink! My guide is astonished at how friendly the dolphins are with us. I smile and continue my silent telepathic conversations with them. Telling them about their brothers and sisters in the oceans of all continents. About my travels. About how happy I am to see them and that I love them. I feel their download of communication to me and watch them gratefully.

My guide thinks they love me and that they must have been my lovers once, because they keep on coming back to our wooden canoe. There is a myth in Brazil about the pink dolphins seducing young women at night, having shapeshifted into human *form, only to return into the river as dolphins in the morning.*

In the evenings, I am happy sitting on the waterside porch, drinking caipirinhas and watching the other dolphins of the Amazon, the little grey river dolphins, the tucuxis, swim by. What bliss!

Another journey:

I am traveling from Nepal to India on the local bus. It is completely full inside. I watch the locals climb onto the roof, sitting between pieces of luggage. They nod to me to do the same. I climb up, thrilled. It is wonderful up there. One of the most beautiful roadtrips I have ever been on; watching the Himalayan panorama pass by on a two-day journey up and down winding, narrow roads, on the roof of the bus.

I often wondered why traveling works so well and is so easy for me. Somehow, when I feel called to do another trip, it happens. If I needed more money, suddenly miraculously another job showed up.

I have been on all continents except to Antartica and traveled to 45 countries to date. Traveling was already part of my childhood, I flew on my first crosscontinental flight when I was 2,5 years, grew up bilingually, in different countries and on different continents.

The answer comes as I am doing a regression, related to a completely different question about healing my inner child.

My eyes are closed and I have entered the invisible world. I see a small child in the woods. She is four or five, playing in the forest next to her family's cabin. Her brothers and sisters are near the cabin, she hears their voices.

I realize I am that small child, even though she looks different than I did as a child now. It is a past lifetime.

Suddenly a rider comes through the forest. He sees the child, quickly rides up to her and with one swoop of his arm brushes her up and onto the horse under his cloak. The child is terrified, he holds her mouth shut with his hand.

He rides a long, long way and time, with several night breaks. Then they reach a castle. The rider brings the child to another man there. He is the lord. He looks at her; then she is taken to another room with other children, different ages. They work there. The child never sees her family again.

As she grows older, the lord takes particular favour in her. She gets her own room, where she is even taught some musical instruments. She is not allowed outside very often, and rarely with the other children. Every so often, the lord comes by, and she plays him music. He talks with her.

So the years go by, and she rarely is permitted out of the castle. She is a prisoner there, the lord's pet. She is unhappy, and doesn't live long, still a younger adult.

As she passes out of her body her last thought is
»Finally I am free.« Her soul travels lightly and
easily to the bardo, the plane of existence before
reincarnating again. She meets her spirit guide
there to review her life's experience and prepare
for the learning steps in the next incarnation. The
spirit guide has been with her for many lifetimes,
aeons.

Her soul says to her guide, »I have made the
experience of imprisonment.« The guide replies,
»And once you will make the experience the
opposite – freedom. You will be able to go
wherever you want to, whenever you want to; you
will be able to travel the entire world.« She nods.
She knows that learning comes in many ways, and
sometimes also in experiencing opposites – such as
being victim and victimizer; rich and poor; ill and
strong, healthy. Karma is never about retribution,
but about experiencing both sides. Life on Earth is
dual, is polarity.

As I slowly come out of the trance, I have not only
made another step to healing my inner child, but
also come to realize why I am able to travel so
much. Often it has felt as if the angels are around
me, helping me to make travel happen and
safeguarding me on the way. Now I know that in
fact it really is so.

Life is here, life is now – and I love it! I am
traveling again, seeing how wondrous and beautiful
this world is. Traveling is like meditation to me,

like spending time in nature or doing yoga: It helps me let go of my daily chores and agendas, I connect with my soul purpose and passion, come into a state of just being again.

I love exploring, life is so short and such a gift. I immerse into the energy of the new place I travel to. It has a consciousness of its own, made up of the history of the place, the collective memory stored there, the stories of all people living there. Traveling brings me back to the source, the wonder and mystery of life.

I am in southern California with a friend, taking a bus to the Mexican boarder. We have decided to hitchhike for the experience, fun and adventure of it. At the Mexican boarder we get off the bus and sit at the side of the road with our backpacks. Waiting and telling stories, laughing, hitchhiker's thumbs up.

It doesn't take long, half an hour or so, and a big pickup pulls up. This is classic. A Mexican man with a big cowboy hat gets out and asks us where we are heading. We tell him we want to eventually get to Mexico City, but are happy for any lift that will take us in that direction. He nods and asks us where we are from. We tell him and smalltalk a little. He is checking us out and we are doing the same. His English is excellent and he seems very pleasant. He has a long drive ahead of him, a day's journey south and offers us to ride in the back of his pickup truck.

We are happy and excited as we climb onto the back of his truck. Pulling on hats and wrapping up under blankets we enjoy the open air ride, watching the Mexican landscape and people pass by.

Hours later, we stop at a roadside stop for some food. All three of us enjoy our conversation, talking about traveling and people. The Mexican, too, has traveled a lot and seen quite a bit of the world.

As we pay to drive onwards, he asks us if we would like to stay overnight at his ranch. His wife and small son are there, we can stay in the guest house. And he has horses he offers us to ride on. We accept happily.

At dusk we arrive at the ranch. It is huge, with many cattle and horses. The house is beautiful and we are warmly welcome by his wife. The little son is really sweet. We are invited to eat dinner with them and instantly all get along.

We stay three days. Their hospitality is overwhelming. We have an entire small guest house to ourselves. We ride on the horses every day.

The Mexican rancher shows me how to ride with just a blanket as a saddle and a simple rope as a halter. He tells me to talk to the horse, it will be easy. And even though I am no expert rider and have only been with horses a few times, it works. I trust what he explains to me, I watch how he does it. And then it is as if the horse and I become one. We gallop over the flat and dusty Mexican landscape, endless space. I whoop and holler, happy, what a beautiful life this is!

The gifts of travel. They are jewels to me, precious, I will always remember in my heart and soul.

I admire the beauty and diversity on our planet. Not only nature but all its beings. Even the creepies and crawlers, the insects, which help turn around the earth and are nourishment for many beings. That's why there are so many of them, at the bottom of the food chain.

I enjoy watching and learning from the insects: the strength and diligence of the ants shimmering red, black, gold and silver. The wonder of a pupa turning into a multicolored butterfly. The gentle rocking motion of a mesmerizing praying mantice. The hundreds of legs on a centipede. The fascination of a spider. A simple brown earthworm. They too are beautiful, some very obvious such as bright butterflies – some only at second glance, such as bugs.

It is the same with human doings, accomplishments and structures. We too are part of nature. Much created by earthlings is amazingly beautiful – some obvious, some at second glance.

Obvious: beautiful music of all centuries and continents, literature, food, art, buildings.

At second glance: small niches in large cities with a multitude and diversity of cultures living door to door, crowded and smelly, but with a fascination and beauty of their own, the richness of colors and languages and people.

More than anything else, I love to experience nature and encounters with people when I travel.

We leave the ranch in Mexico with happy farewells from the rancher and his family. We all know it was a beautiful encounter and we will probably never see each other again.

Our hearts are open with gratefulness. My friend and I travel onward to Mexico City. I stay there a week and then travel further south to Guatemala by myself; my friend decides to stay in Mexico City longer to study Spanish. I think the main reason is because he met a girl in our hostel he likes.

I am glad to be on my own for a while, before my mother comes for a two-week holiday to meet me. When she comes, we stay in a beautiful Guatemalan guesthouse with a friendly owner. He invites us to visit a tiny mountain village with him.

One morning we leave very early to walk several hours up the mountain through the gorgeous lush forest. The village is without electricity, another world. The guesthouse owner is friends with the people there and introduces us. Another heart- and mind-opening jewel of travel.

After my mother departs again, I hang out with some travelers. Then I feel it is time to move on again. And just the next day, as synchronicity often goes, another traveler I made friends with comes and asks me if I feel like sailing on a boat from Lago Isabal through the Rio Dulce to the Carribean coast of Guatemala and down to Honduras. She has befriended two Americans with their teenage son who invite her to sail with them –

and she should bring along somebody. I am thrilled, of course.

We leave a few days later. Like with the Mexican rancher and his family, we all enjoy each other's company. The sailboat takes its course through the magnificent river valley of the Rio Dulce, surrounded by the lush jungle in all its glory and its own symphony of sounds. We cook and eat together, tell stories, jokes, dance a little and are silent too. Watch magnificent nature pass by the boat like on a movie screen.

Sometimes we anchor for sidetrips into smaller riverarms in their dinghy. There, we see howler monkeys which sound like fierce tigers roaring. We watch special birds, the Americans are avid ornitholoigsts. And we simply explore untouched, beautiful nature.

Once, we also stop on the way to visit another American, a friend of theirs. She lives in the jungle in a lovely house with her young daughter. Everything is run with generators. She works as a teacher in a nearby town. We stay overnight in her spacious house, cook together, talk. And drink a lot of wine.

One of the wonders of traveling is the time it gives to simply be with other earthlings, fellow humans. Not watch television – simply have the time to be. It is heartwarming and nourishing to the soul.

The next morning, the American lady takes us to a local hot spring bath in the jungle, next to a beautiful waterfall. We bathe under the waterfall and relax in the hot spring pools.

Again, we sail onwards. This time down the coast, to Honduras. Dolphins occasionally accompany us on the way, surfing on the bow wave.
 There really is heaven on Earth.

»Once a year go someplace you have never been before«, says the Dalai Lama. What did you always want to do sometime? Which place did you want to get to know? Don´t hesitate. If not you, if not now, when then? By visiting new places and doing new things that you have never done before, you open yourself to the wideness and freedom that you carry inside. You leave old trails and broaden your horizon.
 Some years ago, one of my teachers tells the story of The Singing Stone:

A young woman who lived in a village goes to a wise old woman and says: »I heard that somewhere in the world there is a singing stone.« – »That could be, me child«, replies the wise old woman. »I have heard that is so. But you have to look for and find it yourself.«
 So the young woman travels south, until she meets a small mouse. »Can you tell me where I can find the singing stone?«, she asks. »I have heard it exists«, answers the little mouse. »Why don´t you look for it in the West?«
 So the young woman heads west, until she meets a rattlesnake. »Can you tell me where I can find the

singing stone?« - »I have heard it exists«, hisses the snake. »But it is not here. Why don't you look for it in the North?«

So the young woman goes north, until she meets a bighorn sheep. »Can you tell me where I can find the singing stone?« - »The singing stone? Yes, I heard about it«, answers the sheep. »Why don't you look for it in the East?«

So the young woman walks east, as far as the sun rises. And there she meets a hawk. »Please can you tell me where I can find the singing stone?«, she asks. »Ah, the singing stone,« replies the hawk. »Sure it exists. But it is not here. Sorry.« He sees that the young woman is very tired and exhausted, so the hawk says kindly: »You have traveled so long and far now. Why don't you go home and see what happened there while you were away?«

Sadly, the young woman starts heading back. As she approaches her village, she sees that all the people are standing along the road, greeting and welcoming her home. With hesitant steps she approaches them. It sounds like they are singing something.

As she comes closer, she hears what they are singing: »Welcome home, Singing Stone!«

17. Hawaii – Lemuria

The place I spend the most time during my travels is Hawaii. I am there annually, often several times a year and for many months. I go there to meet the dolphins and whales. Because of an incident on my first trip to Hawaii I feel welcome.

I arrive in the evening, exhausted. With my backpack on the backseat of my rental car, I drive through the night to find a spot to pitch my tent. I am unaware of the fact that you can't simply camp anywhere. So I follow my intuition, as always, and take a turn to a lighthouse. Next to it are beautiful trees, a forest. That is where I want to set up my tent.

Nobody else is there, the night is warm. I can hear the ocean's surf far below the cliffs of the lighthouse. I build my tent and go to sleep.

I wake up from a sound. I realize I am still sleeping but awake in my dream. Two beings have entered the tent. They are taller than humans by several heads. I know immediately that they are spirit protectors of Hawaii. They are beautiful male spirit shapes, carrying spears and looking fierce. They appear brave and purehearted to me. I am alert but not afraid.

»Who are you?« they ask. I tell them my name and where I have traveled from. »What do you want here?« is their next question. I tell them I felt called to come here for many years, by the ancient land as well as by the whales and dolphins.

They look at me intently, silently studying me. I feel their spirit-eyes piercing my soul and heart, checking me out, scanning me, just like the dolphins do. Then, suddenly: »You are welcome here«, they say, and disappear. I know I have passed their test.

In the years to come memories return that I have lived in Hawaii and Lemuria many times before. That is why it is all so familiar when I am there. I feel at home. Sometimes, when I drive around the island my heart just billows open with joy, tears rolling down my cheeks out of gratefulness and love for the land, sea and all its beings.

Lemuria is the name of the ancient continent that is meant to have existed about a million years ago and gone under 25,000 years before Christ. The Hawaiian and South Pacific islands are remnants.

When I arrive in Hawaii that first night, I don´t know yet that I will return again and again. That I will eventually work with the islands, the land and ocean, its people and beings there. The spirits that checked me out in my tent knew – and I was granted permission.

I wake up after the two spirit-guards leave. I sit in the darkness of the night in my tent and feel good, safe, protected. It was another powerful opening. I look at my watch and see that it is barely an hour after I pitched my tent and fell asleep – the spirits came immediately. I fall asleep again soon.

The next morning I am awakened by a voice outside my tent. This time it isn´t from the spirit world – it is a ranger on his morning patrol. He tells me that it is illegal to camp here and that I have to leave immediately. I am to go to a state camping ground nearby. So I pack and leave.

Instead of driving to a state campground, I look at the map and see a waterfall marked further inland. My intuition tells me it is the right place to go. It turns out this is true, because I meet a young Hawaiian man selling traditional crafts there – hula skirts and leaf necklaces. He tells me he and his father make them.

We get along well and end up talking for an hour. I tell him where I camped and what happened with the ranger. He laughs. I tell him about my dream, feeling I should do so; that it would be important to share this with him. His eyes get very big and he looks at me curiously, differently than before. »That is very ancient holy land up there«, he says. »You are very lucky, the spirits can also be very unpleasant.«

»In what way?«, I ask him.

»They can make you get lost in the forest, walking in circles forever«, he explains. »Leading you in there, telling you to follow them.« He pauses. »That happened to me and one of my brothers once. We were doing stuff we weren't supposed to back then,« he carries on, »and the spirits taught us a lesson. We both stopped.«

I really like Kai's energy. »Maybe you can come and camp on our land for a while. Sometimes we do that with travelers we like.« He smiles. »Let's go see what my father thinks of that.«

We drive to Kai's father and it is instant liking. Kalani is an elderly and widowed gentleman with silver hair, kind and serious eyes which shine with wisdom. He lets me pitch my tent on his property, near a little freshwater river where I am allowed to bathe. I end up staying there for several weeks.

I think both Kai and his father take my dream as a sign that they should be the ones to introduce me to Hawaii. Kalani says several times that I am very lucky to have seen the spirit guards; they don't show themselves frequently.

He often talks about Hawaiian culture while he is making his crafts. The hula skirts and necklaces are made out of ti leaves, he explains, which is one of the most holy Hawaiian plants. Ti leaves look a bit like banana tree leaves – large and green.

Kalani doesn't only make the crafts for his son to sell to the tourists, but also for his many children and grandchildren. He has 15 children and about three times as many grandchildren. Kalani's children all have regular jobs – except for Kai, who likes the natural life his father lives and is following in his footsteps.

His children regularly visit with their children and their in-laws. Together they celebrate *luaus*, which is a Hawaiian feast. They do this for every occasion with their *ohana*, their family.

There is a *luau* almost every week while I am there. Everybody brings food. Various grandchildren, starting at three years until their teens, wear grandpa's hula skirts out of ti leaves and dance on a little stage he has built. All the relatives applaud and praise them. It is beautiful and heartwarming to experience this.

18. Values of Living

When his family visits, Kalani often tells his grandchildren little stories about the Hawaiian way to live and behave. It is one of his favorite subjects, to live in *aloha* – in a state of love and kindness. Kai watches his father fondly and smiles, telling me that he also grew up with his dad telling him these stories.

In the hours I sit and talk with Kalani, he also talks to me a lot about the Hawaiian values of living – but as an adult, without stories, simply explaining.

»God gave us love. We call it aloha. *We share this* aloha *with each other.* Aloha *is peace and kindness and affection. We use* aloha *to say hello and goodbye. Being Hawaiian means living, being and doing* aloha *each and every day.*

Hang loose, relax and take it easy. Laugh about yourself and be together with others happily. Just like you, the other person wants to be happy. Great power and strength lie in total relaxation. Then you can trust in yourself. And when you trust yourself, you can trust others.

If a person hurts you, forgive them. If you hurt somebody, apologize and never harm them again.

If there is a conflict, make things right. You need to clear things and restore harmony. Where is the problem in you?

Practice forgiveness of your family, relatives, friends, teachers and everybody, including yourself. Once you forgive, you never raise the issue again. Then you are in harmony with yourself and the world around you. Before the sun sets – do this; do ho´oponopono. *It is a daily practice.*

Be considerate, helpful, sincere and humble. Harmonize with nature. Respect and give thanks to the gift of life, to the people and places in your life, things and events. Thankfulness brings more abundance into your life.

Be patient. Give time to kukakuka *– talk story – with another. Especially the elderly and the children.«*

I love listening to Kalani. After I tell him that nobody talked story with me when I was a child, he also starts telling me stories. I feel like a kid. One afternoon, Kalani tells me the tale of Lemuria.

19. The Return of the Rainbow

»There was a time, so it is said in the ancient tales of Lemuria, or Mu, when life on the Earth was paradise. The children were so light and pure that they were able to dance and walk on the rainbows. There was nothing that weighed them down heavily because there was no reason to.

They had everything in abundance: Food in form of plants and fruit, clothing and houses they made from plants. And ohana - friends and family.

So they spent most of their time playing the game of life: having fun and sharing with an open and loving heart.

This time of Lemuria was before what we call the history of mankind. The children of Mu had a direct heavenly link – the rainbow. It was their constant companion. On it, they could visit their ancestors; it was their bridge from the physical to the invisible world, to other dimensions. It was their opening, always there for them.

Then, as all stories go, one day something different happened. Some of the children started taking the game seriously. It was still a game, but a few *started saying that it had rules – otherwise it wouldn't be the »real« game. Each child had certain areas - given to them by the creator - they were good at: making something, cooking, planting, harvesting, singing, drawing, playing a musical instrument, talking with the divine realms.*

In starting to become too serious, however, the children started thinking it was they alone who were doing what they did. They started to forget that it was the source flowing through them, expressing itself through them. And because they thought it was they alone who did whatever it was they were good at, they started to say that it had to be done exactly their way. They made more rules.

Then, the children stopped sharing and started withholding their knowledge and wisdom from each other when it was needed. And so, the first power plays came into being. That is how they became people, no longer the children of the rainbow.

The rainbow above their heads started to fade. More and more power plays came into being. It was the only way the people still had to feel good. They had lost the good feeling that came from sharing, from an open heart, from the connection and link to the creator and from the understanding that there is abundance for everyone. Instead, they could only feel good by feeling superior to others.

And so, in the course of human history, mankind has gone through all different types of power plays: a time when women thought they were superior to men, a time when men thought they were superior to women. They always vaguely remembered the way it had once been before, as children of the rainbow. They tried to have that again with their power games. But the wantig to have and own was the misconception.

At all times, though, there were also many people who were able to connect to the source again - because the source is always here. But this was often dangerous. It made those who were in power feel threatened and become angry – because they only had power to feel better. And so, over the course of history, those who found the pure rainbow connection were often punished or even killed by those in power.

Something called religion also came into being – again full of rules. It was made by people claiming that they alone had the true connection. This caused wars and mass genocides. Other power plays were those of ownership, of race, of education – all twisted ways to feel better.

But there will always be people, so the Hawaiian legend goes, who remember the connection. Many of these, over the milleniums of human history, went underground with their knowledge and passed it on quietly, carefully, so that it would never be lost. Part of their knowledge was the ability to foresee that there would be a time when the children of the rainbow would return, in a new way.

There will be a time when the memory and knowledge will resurface again. It will return in so many people that it will no longer be dangerous to be a child of the rainbow. The knowledge is inside all of us, even in those misusing their power, and can never be lost.

And so, once a certain large number of people remember and are open again for the rainbow connection, it will resurface in even more people. The children of the rainbow will return.

According to the Lemurian and Hawaiian legends and prophecies, this time is now.«

I love this story Kalani shares with me; it sends joyful chills down my back. I tell Kalani that not only the Lemurian legend speaks of this time – many old cultures around the world, such as the Hopi, Mayans, Egyptians and ancient Greeks have similar prophecies that now is the time of the opening.

These legends describe what science has discovered and termed as the »critical mass« for any evolutionary change to occur in a species. When a certain large number of people – or animals or plants – pick up a new behavior or growth pattern, automatically it is adopted by all other members of this species.

Then, people will not have to be afraid of each other anymore. Then, nobody will allow themselves to be manipulated out of fear anymore. No belief system will claim that God means self-sacrifice and you are supposed to suffer in this life so that you can finally be happy in heaven when you die.

Nobody will believe when somebody tries to tell them others know best what is good for them because they have more experience. People won´t be afraid to be happy anymore because you could want it all the time and that isn´t possible. And most of all, nobody will believe those who claim that it is childish to have fun – that it is much better and wiser to be tense and serious all the time.

Kalani and I laugh loudly, happily and uncontrollably.

For me, the easiest way to find my »child of the rainbow« is to swim with the dolphins. When they twirl around me and we play with each other, my heart and soul become light and happy. I remember how life is really meant to be: play, pleasure, love and abundance.

During my weeks camping on Kalani´s land, I spend the mornings at the beach with the dolphins. Usually I drive there very early before the sun rises. I love getting up early in Hawaii. Everybody here does it. Because Hawaii is so close to the equator, there is a cyle of 12 hours daylight and 12 hours night. The sun rises and sets quickly. People make use of the light in the morning hours. It is such a beautiful time of day.

The dolphins are often in the bay then. I drink my tea and eat a small breakfast as I watch them and wait until the sun rises. Then I enter the water to swim and play with them. Sometimes for half an hour, sometimes they also stay several hours. You never know, it is always a surprise.

If they are not there, then I just spend the morning at the beach, relaxing, reading, enjoying. I chat with other people who have come to be with the dolphins. I snorkel and sometimes meet big old sea turtles – the *honus* - in the water.

Because it is winter, the whales are also here, giving birth to their babies in the warm tropical waters. Often I can see them from the shore, breaching, their mighty bodies rising majestically up vertically in the air and then crashing down with a loud thunder and huge splash.

Afterwards I drive to Kalani´s for a rinse in the freshwater river, lunch and a nap. In the afternoons I usually stay with Kai and his father and listen to them, ask questions. Sometimes I go on trips.

One day Kalani gives me a necklace with a wooden carved dolphin. »This is who you are«, he says. I don´t know at the time that I will eventually be working so much with the dolphins. Sometimes other people see what is in you before you do.

It takes me many years to really believe that this is what I am meant to do. It is such wonderful work! This has also been a journey home to myself and to loving myself, that I truly deserve this.

This is what I understand over the years about dolphins. It is a combination of what I learn from my teachers, from internships with dolphin-oganizations, from what I read and research. And from what the dolphins tell me, how I hear them speak.

20. Dolphin Magic

»We are angels and healers of the ocean. That is why millions of people want to see us every year, feel magically drawn to us.

It may be your soul or dreams calling you to us. This is not your imagination, it is real. We communicate with you telepathically.

We make up to five clicks and squeals simultaneously. That way, we create pictoral holograms. That is how we communicate with each other, and that is how we communicate with you. When you have dreams and visions of us, you can trust these pictures. Often we are sending them to you.

Our brain and that of our cousins, the whales, is the largest of any mammal on Earth in relation to body mass. Our thinking and associative part of the brain is 40 percent larger than that of yours, human. Yes, we are smarter than you!

We have a sonar-echolocation communications system with which we can look into you like with X-rays. It is not without reason that all major militaries of this world invest millions of dollars in studying our communications system and sonars every year. They know how advanced it is, they know it is space-age technology and are trying to copy us.

We produce sounds that you cannot hear anymore. But you can feel them if you are sensitive, with your vestibular system and saccule in you ear. These are used for equilibrium and noting very fine movements. The sounds and frequencis we emit are comparable in strength to medicinal ultrasound. The difference is that we are not machines.

With our powerful sounds we stimulate the genetic double helix in your DNA coding. That is where your potential lies dormant; when it is activated, you remember your soul purpose. The largest part of your DNA is not used, about 98 percent. DNA, the blueprint of life, gets activated by sounds and electromagnetic fields such as those generated by us and our cousins, the whales. We switch your genes on more than chemicals or drugs do.

This occurs in our undersea water environment, which is electrochemically similar to human blood serum. Water is an excellent conductor of vibrations and frequences. This enhances the energetic effects.

We also transmit information bioacoustically and electromagnetically, dowloading to you through the water molecules. They also form the electrogenetic matrix of the DNA. These hydroelectric structures are shaped like pyramids, hexagons and pentagons, and direct healing processes.

This download of information and stimulation of the unused parts in your DNA that bring you in touch with your life purpose is why so many humans, after being with us dolphins in nature, oftentimes suddenly change their life or have new energy.

We also help the Earth in this way, oftentimes swimming in geometric formations and patterns like those found in the hydroelectric structures, helping to balance and heal our planet.

We too, like some of you humans, are channels to higher frequency realms. Because we can perceive such high frequencies, we dolphins and whales are beings which are able to move around in the invisible world. We are very close to the matrix, the source, the energy behind everything. That way, when we meet you, we download from there to you.

That is why it is so important to integrate the information you have received after you meet us. Lie down, go into a relaxed and dream state and let your soul do the rest.

This is why so many of you earthlings feel drawn to us. You feel this, you sense that we can help you develop.

At the same time remember that everything is a game. Have fun, enjoy life! You feel good and happy after you meet us. Your endorphines have been released because you have fun with us – and also because we influence your brainstate with our frequencies. That is also why we can help cure depression in humans, which is one of your most widespread illnesses.

Hunting only takes up a small part of our day, and even that we do playfully; it is not work for us. The rest of our day we enjoy each other and life. We surf on waves just like many of you humans. We jump and some of us even spin.

We love joy and fight little. Our younger male dolphins scuffle to test their strength. They do this in small gangs, away from the main group. When they are fully grown and aware of their strength, they peacefully immerse into the pod again.

We never leave our old, sick and weak behind. We also mourn and celebrate. And like you humans, we too have midwives at birth. By example, we help you humans increase your emotional intelligence and become more empathic.

We are a community in which individuality is no contradiction. The ocean is our teacher: there is hardly any gravity, freedom – but with an order. It is normal that we go off wandering and traveling, sometimes for years. We may spend time with other groups, or we may be alone the whole time. When we return, we are welcome.

We love cuddling and making love. When you watch us, you see that we constantly touch each other. It just feels good. Your body, every cell is longing for tenderness and being touched.

Each cell has a heart and when you love, the cores of your cells glow. Everything you experience is stored in your body. Negative experiences that are stored in your cells can cause illnesses if they are not touched with love to relax them again. Give your body this love and tender touch.

You humans are realizing that there are possibly more intelligent beings than you on Earth. That is why you watch us to learn, to remember.

There is even a spiritual movement involving dolphins and whales. But this has always existed. A tribe of Aborigines in northern Australia believe they are direct descendants of us – and in fact they are. Another group there, the ›Dolphin People‹, believe their shaman is a dolphin. The Maoris call us and the whales ›people of the sea‹. Or the ancient Greeks: One of the god Apollo's appearances on Earth was as a dolphin. The famous temple in Delphi was a place were people came for visions and healing.

We help you heal. There is dolphin-assisted therapy – DAT - where handicapped and ill people come to see us.

You are amazed about the well documented case of a small baby which had microcephaly. This is an illness where the skull stops growing. Your modern medicine does not know how to treat this condition.

Two parents brought their baby to be with the dolphins at a DAT program. For one week, a few times a day, three dolphins were with the baby. Of course, the dolphins knew what to do because they could read the energy blocks in the baby by scanning it.

They directed their sonar-frequencies towards the base of the baby's skull and the backbone, repeatedly, every time they were with it. After a week, the baby's skull started growing again.

Our acoustic and electromagnetic effects on your body explain how such remarkable healings occur. We use our natural biotechnology and can heal those near us sonogenetically.

We like to help humans. We guide fishermen in different places around the world to fish swarms. Throughout all times of history, we have always saved swimmers from drowing or from shark attacks. We like you humans and enjoy being with you.

Our medicine for you is joy, love and gentleness. Life is often so harsh in your world. You humans have forgotten how beautiful it is to be gentle and tender, like with a baby. We remind you of that sensitivity and bring fun and peace.

Our breathing is medicine for you too. We use our breath 100 percent because we need it to survive; we are mammals, and cannot breathe under water. We release all tension when we surface and breathe in deeply, to enrich our cells with enough oxygen for when we dive again. We remind you to also breathe deeply and not hold in any stress and fear. Breathe it out!

You can also learn from the way we dive down very deeply and then quickly swim up to the surface. This teaches you how to change unhealthy patterns in your life and gain a different perspective when you're stuck and frozen. It also shows you that you can be both deep in your soul as well as on the surface and playful; this is no contradiction.

Please visit us in nature, where we are free. The movie Flipper *and dolphinariums give twisted information about what dolphins are about and make people insensitive to the environment. Being in dolphinariums is humiliating for us, like a bear chained to a cage and taught to do tricks with a ball. We are used to swimming the sea, wild. It is awful and also causes us to have less than half our life expectancy to be confined to a little pool.*

We also don't like being pet by people we don't know. Our smile is misleading, it is the natural shape of our face. It doesn't mean we like being touched by strangers. Would you like being fondled by people you have never met before?

So when you hear our call, please follow it and see us in our natural home: the ocean. And there, when you swim with us, don't chase us – we swim better!

Please don't touch us when we are near – that will make us swim away again. We will touch you if we want to. We know you are excited and have a longing to be close to us. You can swim in our direction. But then stop – we will come.

Our rhythm is the same like everything on Earth: coming and going, the tides, breath. And like you earthlings – we also retreat if somebody chases you.

It is better if you call us telepathically; we will come. If we don't want to swim with you – you can believe it – we won't!

Be sensitive when we are sleeping. You can recognize this when we swim deep below the surface and in formation, only coming up for short moments to breathe air and then dive down deep again.

Many of your wonder whether we are extraterrestrial beings. It doesn't matter – but yes, we are connected to the stars and star beings, to many planets and constellations. We are connected with everything, just like you; and we remind you of that. Just like you, everything in the universe is alive and has a soul, an essence. Earth is a leg of the journey for all of us; we are floating through the universe together on it.

It is so beautiful, this Earth, this blue planet. Protect and respect and honor our planet, us, water – yourself!

21. Pele Volcano

I read about the atomic tests in the South Pacific Ocean in the newspaper. I am crying, tears running down my cheeks. Just that morning I had such a beautiful encounter with the dolphins.

I watch 20 dolphins in a knot, playing and cuddling with each other, beautifully and peacefully. They continue with their play, not taking notice of me. Then they slowly move towards me and pull me into their knot.

I am surrounded by 20 dolphins, I can feel some of them brushing against me, their breath bubbles tickle my body. They could easily crush or harm me, but never once do I feel fear, they are so gentle. Even though they movearound a lot, they don't hurt me.

I feel completely engulfed by their love and let myself fall into this space, grateful.

As I read the newspapers, I feel a piercing pain in my body. It is as if I myself have been hit by a bomb. I see the dolphins and whales with my inner eye, beautiful fish, colorful coral, so much life: being killed by bombs.

Seventy percent of our planet´s surface is covered with water, the same amount of water as in our bodies, in our blood plasma. We are so connected to everything.

The majority of living beings on this planet are in the water - from wide oceans to deep lakes, from major riverways to dainty creeks. We come from water, are in the water of our mother´s womb for our first 9 months. Water is ancient nourishment, is the primeval mother, is cleansing and purifying.

In harming water, we harm ourselves. We need it to survive. Without water our DNA has not structure, our cells could not communicate with each other.

How could they? Millions of life forms killed in the atomic tests, not to mention the atomic waste which stops healthy life developing for centuries.

I drive to the volcano. I am so angry. Whenever I have to release steam, I go there. What better place is there for that: I am on an island with the most active volcano in the world. During this period in my life, I oftentimes feel angry about the world in general, how conditions are, how people are treated. One of my strongest motors on my path in the past – aside from love - is painful anger. Meanwhile, this anger has decreased and transformed more and more into compassion. But at this point I am furious.

The most active volcanos on Earth are in Hawaii. The highest mountain on the planet is located here, created by a volcano, if you measure from the ocean bottom. The mountain with the largest mass worldwide is located here, created by a volcano. This is a lot of energy – or as it is called in Hawaiian Huna: *mana* - life force energy.

The volcanos are all located around 19,5 degrees latitude, which appears to be a key point in the universe. When you take any sphere – any planet – and draw a three-dimensional-triangle in it, then one of its base corners will be at 19,5 degrees latitude.

On Jupiter, the eye of the storm, which is a huge constant swirling mass of energy big enough to suck up the Earth, is at 19,5 degrees. On Mars, the largest known dormant volcano in our solar system, with a mound three times the size of the base of Mount Everest, lies at 19,5 degrees.

On Earth, aside from the natural volcanoes in Hawaii, the Great Sphinx and the Pyramids of Egypt as well as the ancient Pyramids of the Sun and of the Moon in Mexico were built at 19,5 degrees. These ancient civilizations are known to have had high levels of knowledge about technology, the stars and universe. In Hawaii, at 19,5 degrees, there is a temple called »Pathway of the Gods«. The legend describes that is where the gods landed in their ships from the heavens.

No scientific explanation or theory exists for the phenomenon of 19,5 degrees. I personally believe that it is a natural portal into other spheres, dimensions and the invisible world. This would explain why ancient civilizations built pyramids and temples at this latitude.

In Hawaii, since my first trip there, I often encounter the invisible world and spirit beings. One of my most distinct encounters is now, at the volcano.

I hike across a crater floor. The volcano there is not extinct, but it is safe to walk across it. Before I start, I give Pele an offering. Pele is the goddess living inside the volcano, goddess of fire and passion. She can help a person ignite excitement in life, find one's life purpose and live it fully. I pray to Pele and tell her about my anger about the atomic tests and ask her to help me transform this anger into a more constructive and positive energy.

I am fuming as I walk across the crater. The landscape is a reflection of my inner state: hot steam rising out of vents, lava rock in all shades of black and grey, no plants. It looks like it could be a landscape in hell. I love it; it has its own primordeal beauty.

Somewhere in the middle of the crater, I suddenly feel the presence of several spirits. I can't see them, but I feel them. They tell me to stop and sit on a large rock. Suddenly, pain shoots down the crown of my head through my spine to my buttocks; a good, cleansing pain. The spirits are cleaning my chakras from bottom to top, up and down, like chimney sweepers. They tell me to keep still.

This goes on for quite some time, at least a quarter of an hour. Then, as quickly as they appeared, they disappear. I feel a little numb and sore where they cleared me - but my anger has dispersed. Instead, I feel compassion, peace and love for all beings.

I have an insight that humankind cannot look for scapegoats in trying to create a balance on Earth. Those people testing atomic bombs, creating oil spills or radioactive leaks are, in endeffect, doing this to hoard astronomical amounts of money they themselves will never be able to use in their lifetime. Their actions are out of greed and power gone wrong.

Their fear of loss needs to be taken into account and they need to be told: »You will lose something, but those are only numbers on papers or displays. You won't lose all of it; there will be enough left for you if you work for a better world. Then, any type of living standard is possible for a wide population. There is enough abundance on Earth for everyone.«

I thank the spirits, I thank Pele for this insight and transformation and leave an offering of tobacco. This healing is a deep experience for me.

Even though anger is still in my life at times as a natural and healthy human reaction when things are out of balance or unjust, a huge lump of furious pain has now transformed.

I camp in the Volanco National Park that night. I want to be close to the fire and Pele. That evening, in the darkness, I hike to the flowing lava fields where visitors are permitted. I watch the glowing red lava flow through the black of the night.

Hours later, after all other visitors have left, I take my blanket and lie down, a safe distance from the lava field. Falling asleep, I watch the lava slowly find its way down the mountainside. Hot red molten lava, the primordial soup, turning into solid black volcanic rock. Earth creating itself out of nothingness, out of the everythingsness of the source, becoming visible.

The spirits are not only in Hawaii; they are all around us, just waiting to be called and worked with again. They have been unemployed for a long time because people have forgotten the connection to the source and how easy it is to communicate with them. Often I am surprised, even though I know exactly how it works, how quickly the spirits respond when I call and ask them for help and support. It really works, I can see it by the results in my life and those of others.

This is what many of the entities are here for – to help each one of us on our path. They can guide us in handling challenges and life lessons on the way. And to have spirits support you on your path is fun.

This path is also about learning to be in balance with yourself and existence. Inherent in all humans are feelings of not only love and joy, but also of pain, anger, hatred and greed. I also struggle with thesw, especially when I think I am right and that the other person is wrong. This is part of being a human being; everybody goes through this and it never stops completely, even when wisdom comes with the years.

The moment I accept these feelings and don´t fight them anymore, they melt. In his song »Second Chance«, singer-songwriter Miten sings about this:

»Embrace your anger, your lust and your greed, that´s how we drop the things that we don´t need.

Make peace with your mother and your father, too, make peace with the stranger inside of you.

And we all come and go like waves in the sea, each with our own responsibility, to leave this world more beautiful than we found it.«

Aside from going to Pele and the volcano, one of the best ways for me to let go of my negative emotions and steam is in the sweatlodge.

22. Pouring Water

»The universe loves abundance and diversity; its infinite creations are a reflection of it. So after it made planet Earth, it sent down one of its helpers to create life to inhabit the beautiful blue planet.

The helper started with the rocks and minerals - crystals and stones of all colors and shapes. Next came the plants – trees and fruit, bushes, flowers, vegetables, healing herbs. Then the animals were created – the creepies and crawlers, those with wings, those in the water, and those on all fours on land. Earth became even more beautiful, so full of life. Next, the helper created humans. They too, came in many different shapes, sizes and colors.

The helper loved the beauty on this planet so much, that it asked the source if it could stay and live here. The source – whose wish it is that all life may exist in abundance and joy – happily granted this. So the helper lived amongst the humans. Together they enjoyed the abundance of good food on the planet. They built homes to provide them warmth and they were in harmony with everything and everyone around them. They enjoyed each other's company, loved one another and flourished. And so, a long time passed.

At some point, however, the helper noticed that something had changed. Somehow it didn't feel so good anymore. As it thought about why, it found the answer. Where all people previously had healthy and strong bodies, now there were illnesses. Where once there existed love and openess, sharing and community, now there was anger, jealousy, greed, even hate. Where once those wonderful minds were full of clarity and understanding, now confusion and doubt took over.

But worst of all, the helper observed, where once there was the connection to the source, with the memory where they had originally originated from, the people had now lost this connection. They even forgot that it existed. They forgot about the divine.

The helper was very sad when it noticed these changes. It went into the mountains to ask the source what to do. After walking a long time, it found a small cave to settle in. It sat at the entrance, looking down the mountainside into the valley.

There, seeing all of Earth's beauty from above, it asked the great mystery what had happened. But no answer came. It was confused by this, because the source had always spoken to it, had even sent it to Earth to create life on it. It asked again what it could do. Again no answer came.

The helper fell into a deep depression. It sat there for many hours and days, again and again trying to *find the connection to the source, praying for an answer. But still, nothing came.*

The days became colder, so the helper had to light a fire in the small cave. It closed the entrance with some blankets to keep the cool air outside. It sat there, alone by the fire, but still no answer came from the source. This became too much for it to bear and it burst into tears, crying and sobbing deeply.

Its tears splashed onto some hot rocks next to the fire and steam rose up. The steam felt good, as did the tears. And it cried more onto the rocks, and more steam rose up. It became very hot in the small cave. The helper started singing and praying, calling the source in this way, putting healing herbs on the fire.

As it sweated, not only its tears came out, but all other bad feelings and thoughts inside of it. And as it sweated, suddenly it could hear the source again. First just a whisper, but soon loudly and clearly.

»You have found the answer to your calling«, the source said. »Sweat in this way with the people, so that their bodies may become purified, their emotions cleansed, their minds cleared. Then, they will hear and remember me again.«

The helper was overjoyed and thanked the source. It returned to the people and told them what had happened. From then on, the people met regularly in the sweatlodge.«

We are sitting in the sweatlodge now and my teachers have just told this story. The sweatlodge is a small, round structure built out of branches and covered with several layers of blankets. There is a hole in the middle in the ground. In it, glowing hot rocks are placed from a large fire outside. On these rocks, herbs are sprinkled and water poured.

It is damp, crowded, completely dark and steaming hot. The sweatlodge symbolizes the womb of mother earth, a sacred space. By entering it and sweating and praying, we become purified and reborn, like a newborn baby. Your mind, body, emotions and soul get reset: You are good; you are loving, loveable and loved.

I have been going to sweatlodges for years. Now I am learning to be a water pourer myself - one who is allowed to pour water onto the hot rocks and helps the people sweat and purify. By doing this, I too cleanse and heal.

In the *Inipi*, as the sweatlodge is also called, we strengthen and cleanse the body. We pray for health for ourselves as well as for others and for Earth - her plants, stones and animals. We ask for healing for what we do to the Earth and ourselves: violence, wars, domestic violence. Everybody can scream in the sweatlodge. This is a great release for most people to let it all out, in the protection of the darkness, where nobody can see them shout and cry.

Then we imagine the Earth in its beauty, strength and glory – as well as all beings and plants and people on it, including ourselves. We promise to look after each other.

We who pour the water, says the teacher, are no better than the participants – it is just our role. We all sit in a circle. Every person has different things to give and to learn, also the water pourer.

That is how the balanced way of all leaders is meant to be; of politicians, healers, doctors. Those who are spokespersons and in power. That is what it means to be in balance with the source: we are a circle, with no beginning, and neverending.

The next day, as part of the training, I spend all day in nature to be close to the source. We undertake such day-long medicine-vision walks, as they are called, numerous times. They are not really a hike but more letting yourself drift, guided by your own inner wisdom and intuition. You walk in the holy space of mother Earth. You are in the invisible, the spirit world. The Earth has much medicine in store for you when you open yourself to her and read in her book of nature. We ask the source specific questions during every medicine walk, such as what we have to heal in ourselves or what our next steps are to pour water, and so forth. Today, the question is whether this is really meant for us. I have asked myself this question many times; there is a lot of responsibility as well as hard physical work in being a water pourer.

23. Animal Medicine

I am on a medicine walk and soon see a large group of deer. They are on the other side of a forest clearing. I stop. We look at each other for minutes. I feel their gentleness, their alertness.

»Be gentle«, they tell me. »Be present and alert, aware, of what is happening in the sweatlodge. Your gentleness, your femininity is your power, your gift.« Then they run into the forest. Deer remind me of the dolphins, who too can disappear so quickly into the ocean´s nothingness.

I walk on, and soon hear the piercing call of a falcon. I look up and see the beautiful bird flying into the forest near to me. I go in that direction. After a few minutes, I spot it perched on a branch above the ground. I watch it, not wanting to frighten it. The falcon is aware of me but doesn´t fly away. It sits with a slanted head, moving it sometimes.

»Come here«, it tells me. Slowly I walk towards the falcon. I sit down nearby, looking up at it on the branch. It is looking down at me, and doesn´t appear to be nervous at all.

One of my teachers said that when you walk in nature in a holy way - as a prayer asking for guidance from the source - the animals will feel that you too are in a different vibration. They will come closer to you than usual, sensing you are connected to the source and to them in a good way.

I have made this experience again and again. Once, while I was leading a midsummer solstice ceremony with a group of people in the forest, a deer and its baby approached us. They remained just a few feet away from us during the entire ceremony. As soon as it was over, they behaved the way deer – especially with their young – usually do: They ran away.

Now, as I sit and watch the falcon, suddenly another one swoops down and lands next to it. They are looking at me. I receive a teaching from them, a download of knowledge and information. That I am on the right path, I am meant to do this. They give me my medicine name.

This is a name that tells you your healing and soul qualities – the real you inside of you. It can come to you in many ways, from nature or from teachers. It is a valuable gift, and should be treated as such, with much love and care. You yourself must decide whom you want to share it with.

I sit in gratitude, hearing what else the falcons tell me. Animals are messengers. They give signs, bring you talents and solutions through their own inherent qualities. They strengthen the instinctive elementary power in all of us. You are connected with feral, instinctual powers. We can learn much from animals. Which animals appear to you? Look at their qualitites and capabilities. They have a message for you. This is what animal medicine and power aninmals are.

Every person is connected to one or several power animals. This is like a good friend, an invisible friend, always by your side. It is part of and always with you. It can be any animal – its size is not important. A butterfly is tiny – yet it has the great animal medicine of lightness and lucidity.

Important is that you have good contact and talk freely with your power animal. When you are afraid or in a difficult situation or feel weak, you can call your power animal. It will be there immediately to help, strengthen and protect you.

The falcons above my head tell me to soar up and see my life from a higher perspective; to use their wings to fly up from what can sometimes become the heaviness of human existence. I sing their song to them:

> *Fly like an eagle*
> *Flying so high*
> *Circling the universe*
> *With wings of pure light*
> *With wings of pure love*

They rise, together, and fly away.

I received many answers. I experienced another opening, to be allowed to pour water in the sweatlodge. Permission can only come from the source – that is what our teachers taught us. They, as our teachers, can give us all the skills, prepare us for all eventualities and show us where we can improve. But we have to find the connection to and permission from the source ourselves. You can´t get a diploma for that.

24. Crossroads

During the time of my sweatlodge training, I am still working as a radio music and talkshow host. It is an interesting job which I do for over six years, along with four colleagues.

The program is three hours long, daily and about world music and culture. Its goal is integration and increasing cultural awareness.

I meet interesting artists, musicians and activists from all around the world. Many of them are famous, such as Buena Vista Social Club, Angelique Kidjo, Noa and Giora Feidman. It is meaningful work to me, opening the minds and hearts of the listeners.

But, as in every field in journalism, there are policitics involved with those running the show. My boss backs my style as do many others. The »upper« programming level cautions us to keep the show light and not go too deep - as to not overchallenge the listeners.

I often hear this in all fields of journalism I work in - print, radio as well as television: Do not overchallenge the listeners, viewers and readers. I never cease to feel irritated by such guidelines. It sounds to me like it is assumed that the consumer is, in the end, not particularly bright.

My path has always been of depth and truth. It is my nature; except during playtime, I am not interested in anything but authenticity.

I believe that the readers, listeners and viewers are intelligent and know exactly if something rings true or not. They can sense if information is being witheld from them

This is, six years, my ongoing challenge at the radio station. It is a popular station with educated listeners. Even though they often write fan letters or call appreciating and praising my style, the »highest« station levels within its hierarchical structure advise me again and again not to get too poltical, too spiritual.

I find it extremely difficult not to ask political or spiritual questions when a choire of 10 Tibetan Buddhist monks touring the world to increase awareness of Buddhism and the Tibetan political situation are my guests. Or with Pakistani Sufi musicans whose entire musical tradition is based on a spiritual living practice. Oftentimes, musicians start talkig about politics or about spirituality by themselves. My boss always gives the okay; he backs me and is political himself.

After years of working at the station, I feel the time has come to move on. I have reached a dead end, this road won´t take me any deeper into what I am interested in.

I always keep on traveling to the dolphins and whales and doing trainings in reiki, shamanic healing, the sweatlodge and so forth. Maybe now is the right time to work in this field, starting with shiatsu – japanese acupressure. But at the same time I am unsure if it is not too soon. I have great respect for this work.

During this time, I have another strong opening one night.

I am sleeping. I wake up in my dream from a presence behind me. Two of them come to my side, where I can see them. They are small beings in robes. I have seen them before as a child when my star family visited me. Again, I feel safe, loved and good.

They do something with my head. It feels like they are opening the top of it. There is no pain, just an intense tingling and a sense of my crown popping open. They hold some kind of device there, like a funnel.

Suddenly I see the entire universe. It is immense and beautiful. It all flows into my head, the entire vastness and diversity. I am completely expanded, open, loving, trusting.

This goes on for some time. Then they close my head again. The star beings disappear into nothingness.

I awaken immediately. I sit up in bed, touching my head. It is warm and throbbing lightly. A thought enters my mind that not only each person is a part of the universe – but that the universe is also always within each one of us. I feel safe, strong, protected. I fall back asleep.

The next day, I have another show. My guest is from Brazil, a musician, part of whose proceeds go to orphanaged and homeless slum children. The musician wants to talk politics. Worried, I look at my boss through the studio window. We know each other well over the years, he understands me nonverbally. He gives me the thumbs up – to go ahead. I know he will back me when the »upper« level comes later.

And so it is. After the show, the programming chef comes down to talk with my boss. I know what their discussion is about behind closed door – it is always the same.

Usually, I am nervous and worried. But this time I am relaxed, at ease. I feel the opening from the night, remember what happened – and understand. It is the go-ahead for me to quit my job. That I will be safe in my new field. They have downloaded knowledge and information and I am ready and prepared.

I enter the room where my boss and his boss are talking - and quit, telling them it is time for me to move on. My boss tries to persuade me to stay, but at the same time understands my decision.

After finishing my contract, I travel to the dolphins and whales for some time. After returning and starting with shiatsu and reiki, I immediately have clients. I soon include the sweatlodge and shamanic healing work. A few years later I start bringing people to the dolphins and whales.

The abundance in clients has never stopped; often my groups are full with waiting lists. I love this work and am grateful to be able to help the heavens bring more light, love and healing on this planet, our Earth.

I look back on my ten years working succesfully as a journalist in the fields of print, radio and television with pride. They were interesting. But I don´t miss them. Life is always changing, it is good to flow with these changes, not get stuck in a rut.

After a few months of working in my new field, I meet my old boss. He has always been fatherly towards me and looks at me worried.

»How are things going?« When I tell him everything is developing wonderfully, he looks relieved and surprised at the same time. How could I tell him about the star family which visited me the night before I quit, and that I knew everything was going to be allright?

25. Star Beings

Star beings exist, there is no doubt. The world political, scientific and economic arenas are starting to adjust to this reality.

The United Nations, for example, in 2010 appointed an official for first contact with extraterrestrial life. It stated the reason for this due to the discovery of an Earth-like planet in the universe in the same year, officially announced by the National Science Foundation. This makes it more likely than ever that humanity will eventually discover other life than that on Earth.

Astronomers have long spoken about the statistical probability to eventually discover such a planet. There, in the socalled Goldilocks zone, key conditions for life to exist are just right and habitable. Not too far from their main sun or star, not too close. So it´s not too hot, not too cold for liquid water and life. It´s just right. Just like Earth.

Scientists working on the Kepler Space Telescope announced that rocky Earth-like planets are more prevalent than gas giants such as Jupiter and Saturn. This has fueled scientific speculation that suitable life-bearing conditions are far more common than previously thought.

This was confirmed by the NASA telescope, that in 2011 spotted more than 50 potential planets that appear to be in the habitable zone – just a year after the first Earth-like planet was discovered. In just this one year of peering out into a small slice of the galaxy, the Kepler telescope discovered 1,235 possible planets outside our solar system, of which 54 are seemingly in the zone that could be hospitable to life.

NASA´s Charles Bolden said: »In one generation we have gone from extraterrestrial planets being a mainstay of science fiction, to the present, where Kepler has helped turn science fiction into today´s reality.«

And again, ancient indigenous cultures have known this all along: The old Native Indian cultures of North and South America speak of 12 planets with human-like life in other solar systems. Further they describe 144 paralell universes.

Not only indigenous cultures are known to communicate with star beings; contact with extraterrestrial spirits for their wisdom and power has also been a long term project for secret societies.

Many cults such as Freemasons, Order of Templi Orientis and Scientology claim to be guided by spirits of extraterretrials who are referred to as the Secret Chiefs or Hidden Masters.

Some ancient texts also talk about how to make contact with other parts of the universe. For example the Kabbalah, the ancient mystical school of Judaism, teaches about parallel universes which intersect with our own reality on Earth and make contact with extraterrestrial lifeforms possible.

France was the first country to open its files on UFOs in 2007. Its national space agency unveiled a website documenting more than 1,600 sightings spanning five decades. These cases are visible in their online archives and are updated as new cases are reported.

Of those 1,600 cases registered since 1954, nearly 25 percent are classified as type D, meaning that »despite good or very good data and credible witnesses, we are confronted with something we can´t explain.«

Following France´s example to open their files on UFOs are a long list of countries (and the United Nations), which is constantly growing. To date: United Kingdom, Canada, New Zealand, Brazil, Denmark, Finland, Mexico, Peru, Russia, Spain, Sweden, Uruguay, Argentina, Australia, China, France, Germany, India, Ireland, Japan, Ukraine, United Nations, Vatican City, Chile.

The question whether star beings actually exist has until now been confined to esoteric discussions between intellectuals, researchers and experiencers of extraterrestrial encounters on the fringes of mainstream academia. This is now changing rapidly. World famous British physicist Stephen Hawking started the official academic contemplation about other lifeforms in the universe in a 2010 documentary series on the *Discovery Channel*.

Also, in the same time period, both the Vatican and the Royal Society of London held fullblown astrobiological conferences about the implications of life found in other worlds. Princeton University announced a »Planets and Life« certificate program in astrobiology. It offers students an interdisciplinary approach to the possiblity of extraterrestrial life.

Aside from Earth-like planets in the universe, there is the likelihood that lifeforms also exist on non-Earthlike planets in the galaxy that have completely different biological structures.

The largest known star, for example is VY Canis Majoris (Red Hypergiant). This star has a diameter of about 1,739,839,331 miles or 2,800,000,000 kilometers. How can you imagine this size?

Think of a passenger airplane flying along the surface of this star at about 600 mph or 900 km/h. It would take 1,100 years to circle it one time. Yet it is only a tiny dot among several hundred billion stars forming our galaxy. And there are a hundred billion galaxies out there.

A planet is but a cell in the universe, a person but an atom. Just as our body has veins, the veins of our Earth are her rivers, and the veins of the universe are its galaxies such as the Milky Way.

All this has led to the realization that due to the advanced age of some solar systems, older and more advanced intelligent life very likely can be found elsewhere in the galaxy. The question here is: Have these civilizations learned from mistakes and become more benign, wise and peaceful? Or is evolution on alien worlds likely to be Darwinian, which may mean extraterrestrials share human´s tendencies for violence and exploitation?

I assume both is the case – just like on Earth. Here, there are individuals as well as countries that have learned from past mistakes – whereas others have not yet and are repeating exploitation and genocide.

Maybe, the fear of many people of extraterrestrial life in the universe will bring humankind together as one family. Regardless of our differences, in heart and soul we are one.

In any event: star beings too – as alien they may seem – have a soul, like everything in the universe.

Meanwhile on Earth, as is human nature, business too is starting to come into the picture to reflect on the implications of possible foreign life in the universe. The first business forum that discussed UFOs and extraterrestrial life was the Global Competitiveness Forum. It is hosted anually in Saudia Arabia and started years ago as a gathering of IT experts, which included Bill Gates. Business trends and insights essential for future business investment and competitiveness are discussed.

In 2011 a panel was titled »Contact: Learning from Outer Space« and featured renowned astrophysicist Michio Kaku, together with UFO experts Stanton Friedman and Nick Pope.

Considering that so many people have seen UFOs as well as extraterrestrials, why don´t star beings show themselves to a larger public? For me, the answer is clear: I wouldn´t show myself to a larger public either, knowing the history of humankind. Every country – without exception - which has discovered other nations on Earth has ended up conquering and destroying it.

It is not surprising that most Hollywood movies about star beings are worst-case scenarios with dangerous aliens invading Earth to conquer it. These movies are a reflection of humans´ biggest fear that the same will be inflicted upon them which they have done to others in the past.

Star beings with the intelligence to travel to our Earth from their worlds most certainly observe and study humans as well as our history. They know why they are not showing themselves to a larger public. Most likely that which the humans are so afraid of – being attacked by aliens – would happen to them if they showed themselves peacefully.

26. Starseeds

There are many people who have peaceful feelings about star beings and experienced peaceful encounters with them. Some even feel to be more star being than human.

There is a term for such people: »starseeds«. Books have been written about them and some of them meet on internet forums or in workshops.

They often feel foreign on this planet. Starseeds sense that they either have not been here often yet or that this is their first time. Often, they also feel like they don´t belong to their physical Earth family.

I remember my childhood encounter with my star family:

»I was once your father – and am it still«, says one of the beings to me. »You can always connect with me for guidance, love, support.« I look at the tall, bluish figure and know it is true.

»Your mother and brother on Earth are also connected with us. Your biological father is not. He has a different origin. But he made it possible for you to incarnate on Earth, to learn and grow.

That is why we make sure, in the DNA, that star children look more similar to the parent on Earth they are not connected to on a deep soul level, to the parent who is primarily a biological provider. That way, that parent will not reject its child when he starts to notice how very different it behaves, thinks and talks.

At the same time, through such experiences, both the child and the parent learn how different we all can be and that this diversity is good. Always remember: We all come from the same source. It is about acknowledging differences, respect.«

I wonder whether it is like this for all children. I am thinking about some of my classmates.

»No«, one of the star beings answers. »There are also star children on Earth with both parents being soul as well as biological parents, or star children with both parents biological parents but not on a soul level.«

Starseeds like the Earth as a planet and find it beautiful. But the stars and universe fascinate them and they feel that is where they come from, their original home. Some can remember where from, some not.

Usually, starseeds have a hard time understanding how society here, its structures and governments work and find these crude, primitive and brutal. They question these and are often active in creating alternatives to conventional ways in all areas of life such as medicine and technology, agriculture, politics and culture.

Many starseeds feel they are here for a reason, to help the Earth evolve to a higher and peaceful level of being, a new frequency. That they have advanced knowledge in many areas, and are here to share their expertise. The concept of life in other galaxies is natural to them, also of interstellar travel and of space travel technology. Many starseeds, but not all, have memories of these.

I feel I am also a starseed. And at the same time, I am a normal human being with hopes and worries, strengths and weaknesses, a longing for love, friendship and fun in life.

Everybody – whether earthling or beings in different galaxies – carries the spark and seed of the source in them. Everyone and everything has a soul. Everybody is here to shine on that part of universe where they are living.

And everybody is a starseed. We have also been incarnated on others planets. But some have been incarnated on Earth so many times, that the memory has faded.

If you have memories of other places in the universe, or if you travel there sometimes in your dreams – there is a valuable message there for you. This is information about your life, and be it that you are loved by and at home in the universe.

When I started remembering, one of the details that surfaced was that I was from somewhere around Sirius. This name, this information was simply there, out of the blue. It literally came out of my blueprint in my soul, I believe today. I didn´t

»know« a thing about Sirius. It was a name and a place in the sky and anyhow I was on Earth now.

It wasn´t until years later that I read an interview with author and spiritual teacher Drunvalo Melchizedek. In it, he explained that dolphins and whales originally came from Sirius B, companion star of Sirius A. This information struck me like lightning and I started researching.

Sirius A is one of the brighter stars in the night sky which can be seen from almost anywhere on Earth with the naked eye, whereas Sirius B can only be seen with a telescope.

Bright Sirius A is represented in nearly all ancient world cultures. It is linked to Osiris in ancient Egypt, to mythology in ancient Greece and legends in China, Japan, the Arab countries, Scandinavia and with the American Hopi Indians, just to name a few.

The most fascinating reports about old wisdom about Sirius A come from the Dogon tribe in Mali, western Africa. Their knowledge speaks not only of Sirius A, but also about its companion star Sirius B.

As the story goes, in the late 1930s four Dogon priests revealed their tradition to two French anthropologists, Marcel Griaule and Germain Dieterlen. These spent 15 years living and studying the tribe. The myth they told the two French men was about the star Sirius and its companion star, which are to them the origin of their gods and life.

The Dogon priests said that the companion star is invisible to the human eye. They also explained that it moved in a 50-year elliptical orbit around

Sirius. That it is small and heavy and rotates on its axis.

All of this has been confirmed by modern science. This imformation would normally be considered impossible without the use of telescopes. According to Marcel Griaule´s books *Conversations with Ogotemmeli* and *The Pale Fox*, the Dogon knew about this far before western astronomers discovered the companion star Sirius B in the 1920s.

Furthermore, the Dogon have ancient cave drawings depicting large figures in astronaut-type helmets and clothing. Their mythology says that the gods came from Sirius B – which they call *Po Tolo*, meaning »star creation« -, and joined with the Dogon to help them. They had children with the Dogon.

The tribe also highly reveres water. This is understandable considering they live in a landlocked desert area far away from the ocean. What however is fascinating is that they have cave paintings of dolphins and also call them gods. Coming from where according to their mythology? You guessed it: Sirius B.

So when I researched all this, I was dumbfounded. It was the first explanation I came across for feeling so strongly connected to dolphins and star beings from the vicinity of Sirius.

27. Everybody comes from the Stars

That everyone is a starseed and has star being in them is indicated by numerous indigenous and other ancient cultures as well as human evolution.

Until about 50,000 years ago, the development of humans progressed stepwise. This is scientifically commonly accepted based on archaeological findings. Each phase of human development started at a higher level than the previous one; but once a new level was attained, further development was slow.

Then, suddenly, change occurred at a much greater speed. This is termed as the »Great Leap Forward« or »The Big Bang of Human Consciousness«, for which no scientific explanation exists.

Putting it in words on the yardstick of human development: For hundreds of thousands of years mankind lived in caves – and suddenly he was creating buildings in unsurpassed architecture and beauty such as the pyramids in Egypt or ancient Mayan temples in Latin and South America.

The transition for mankind to have learned this was hardly there, in relation to the scale of past developments. Suddenly buildings were made out of material incredibly large and heavy. Some of the blocks in the Egyptian pyramids weigh over 10 tons, which is as heavy as 10 passenger cars. What kind of technical devices or cranes put them there?

Nan Madol is a ruined city that lies off the eastern shore of the island of Pohnpei in Micronesia, northeast of Australia. Its 80 buildings were built out of 400.000 basalt columns, many of them 10 meters high, 12 meters long and weighing 10 tons.

In many of these sites stone so hard was used, that no simple rock, bone or even metal tools could make precise holes and lines in it. But in Pumapunku in Bolivia, for example, eighth-inch-precise lines and holes were drilled in a way that only modern sophisticated diamond tools could. The holes and lines appear to have been used for some type of technical device; for what, remains unclear.

What happened with mankind during this timespan of approximately 40,000 years? A gigantic leap took place for which science has no explanation.

Answers can be found in the legends, paintings and ceremonies of ancient indigenous people, as well as in other old cultures. Many describe gods and beings coming from the skies in flying objects and having offspring with humans. Drawings and artwork depict astronaut-like looking beings and flying objects.

The First Book of Moses talks about sons of god coming from the skies and making children with the human daughters. The Semitic Lamech scriptures talk about the »guardians of the skies«.

There are legends in Peru and Bolivia about a golden boat coming from the sky.

»Even though there was not a cloud in the sky, the Earth shook from thunder as the boat landed in Lake Titicaca. The goddess of the sky came forth from the boat and had children with the strongest men. Then, one day, she left again with her golden bark. It rose into the sky and disappeared.«

There are similar tales in Tahiti and other islands of French Polynesia.

The Hopi Indians of Arizona have a myth of non-human gods they call *kachinas* coming from the skies to help them. They lived with them for a long time and had offspring with the Hopi. Then, suddenly, they left and said they would return one day.

The Hopi have figures and rituals depicting exactly what the kachinas looked like, so that their children are not afraid of them when they return. Fascinating is that they look very similar to modern-day astronauts – with bulky suits and helmets. Their ancient cave-paintings also depict kachinas with what look like technical devices and machines.

Similar myths and depictions of astronaut-like deities exist amongst the Kayapo Indians in the Brazilian Amazon jungle. They too have a legend of gods who came with a thundering weapon which could put any man to ashes instantly. In their dances and ceremoinies, the deities wear a *bo*, which again, looks like an astronaut suit.

The oldest photographs from anthropologists of a *bo* are from 1952 – many years before the first astronauts circling Earth wearing spacesuits became public.

A similar suit and mask are worn in Papua New Guinea in ceremonies, with similar legends.

The question arises if star beings would indeed have developed a similar physique as mankind in order to be able to mate. According to science – if these beings developed in the Goldilocks habitable zone on Earth-like planets – the answer is yes. If there are similar external conditions, then the living beings there will develop with a similar physique and organs. This would make it theoretically possible for them to crossbreed with humans from Earth, even if they are genetically a different species.

How would travel through such huge distances in space from distant galaxies be possible? Albert Einstein offered the explanation with his theory of relativity and the spacetime lag.

If you fly in a very fast spacecraft out of the Earth´s atmosphere, time passes slower than on Earth. For example, if you move for 50 years in a spacecraft, on Earth 420,000 years will have passed.

With advanced technology, scientists say, it would be possible to build photon-powered spacejets traveling at the speed of light where these spacetime lags occur. Calculations for this exist.

Evidence of this kind of spacecraft technology from star beings visiting Earth can also be found in all cultures. The Australian Aborigines have a legend of the goddess of the Milky Way coming and helping and leaving offspring with them. There are depictions of her with spacecraft-looking objects in ancient cave paintings.

The aboriginal boomerang also may be evidence of a more advanced intelligence having visited. Nowhere in nature can its aerodynamic form be found to copy from or develop. Highly technical knowledge was at work here, for when you throw a boomerang and it misses its goal, it returns to the person throwing it.

In 1909 the inventor David Unaipon developed a rotary wing aircraft based on his study of boomerang aerodynamics. From this, modern-day helicopters were developed.

Clearly, a high intelligence was at work to introduce the boomerang to the Aborigines 30.000 years ago. Similar boomerangs were also found in ancient Egypt, Europe and the Americas.

Ancient Sumerian art – in modern Iraq - depicts a multitude of aircraft-like objects, balls in the sky and gods with torches on their back. It can be assumed that this artwork is naturalistic – showing what they actually saw – because the artforms of all cultures started naturalistic and became abstract later, without exception.

In Egypt of the same era, large numbers of wing-like beings were made. There is even a wooden airplane which is over 2,000 years old. It looks like a model of a sailplane and, if built on a larger scale, is capable of flying.

China also has several ancient paintings of flying objects with beings in them. And in Columbia old golden jewelry shows flying objects with aerodynamic principles.

The Mayan ruins of Palenque in Mexico not only depict flying objects, but also detailed technology. There is, for example, an astronaut-like figure pressing a pedal with both hands and feet. This, as well as the few Mayan scriptures that were saved from being destroyed by the Spanish invaders, shows astronaut-type figures with what look like modern-day flashlights, oxygen tanks and engines.

Finally, the ancient Nazca Lines of Peru could be evidence of landing places for such aircrafts. These lines are so huge, so wide and long, that they can only be recognized from high up in the sky. They cover a large part of the plateau of Nazca.

There is evidence right in our brains and genes that we might be hybrids between humans and star beings. Some DNA researchers believe that extraterrestrial genes – and knowledge - are embedded within the 97 percent of human genomes as yet described as junk or dormant DNA – because scientists never knew what it was used for.

British molecular biologist Francis Harry Crick, who won the Nobel Prize for the co-discovery of a double helical structure for all our DNA, claims that based on the structure of DNA, life arrived on Earth from somewhere else in our solar system.

The largest parts of the brain are still not understood by scientists. Our brain consists of 80 percent water with 100 billion nerve cells. This high performance computer out of water takes care of all cells and functions in our body and never sleeps.

Nerve cells in our body create 1,000 connections to other neurons. These can simultaneously perform 200 operations per second, which would be a computing power of 10 teraflops – about the data amount of 2,100 DVD movies running simultaneouly within 1 second. The memory capacity of the human brain is 1-4 petabytes – about 1 million gigabyte.

With that, even if we were several 100 years, we could remember every single of the 11 million sensory perceptions that enter us unfilitered every second. Burned on a CD-ROM and stacked, these 4 petabytes would make a tower of approximately 6,8 million CDs with a height of over 9 miles or 16 kilometers – almost double as high as Mount Everst. Who helped make this brain?

Something is drawing us out into space – human evolution and technological space development are moving in exactly that direction, as if an undertow were pulling us out there.

Just 200 years ago man flew the first time – now we have space travel. Dormant knowledge in our DNA is possibly awakening to support these huge developmental jumps.

Old indigenous wisdom says that not only humans have part star origin. According to them, the whales and dolphins are the only other beings on Earth who too partially come from other planets and stars.

Whether the Dogon in Africa, the Hopis and other Indian tribes in the North and South Americas and various Aboriginal groups – they describe whales and dolphins as not being from this world. So high is their intelligence, wisdom and compassion.

Swimming with the dolphins and whales in their world often feels like visiting star beings on a different planet.

This is what I heard over the years from the whales. It is a combination of what I learned from my teachers and from what I read and researched. And from what the whales have told me, how I listenend to them speak.

28. Whale Magic

»We are the largest ones on Earth. Even bigger than the largest dinosaurs that once existed. We grew so well because we have room, space to expand in the oceans.

The entire Earth and all its oceans are our home. Some of us swim on a journey around half the globe and back every year.

We can swim down very deep. Sperm whales can stay underwater without breathing for two hours and dive to a depth of 1,5 miles or 2,000 kilometers.

The largest of our kind is the blue whale, the size of a boeing jet. Its heart is the size of a car and 50 people could stand on its tongue. A bus would have enough room to drive into its mouth.

And yet the blue whale is so gentle and only eats krill.

We are gentle giants and that is our medicine for you: to be peaceful and gentle warriors of light. Don't abuse power and strength but instead use it for light.

Each of you has power, strength, grandness. Every one of you is capable of working for the light.

We also work for light using our frequencies and songs. We communicate over thousands of miles and kilometers, that is how powerful our vibrations are. When a humpback whale sings, it has the sound force of a boeing jet taking off.

We also communicate with Mother Earth. We create a grid of light-frequency to balance and hold her. Many of us swim in the pattern of an infinite eight on our yearly journey from the poles to the equators and back. This is because we create a grid of light-frequency with our songs in this swimming pattern:

You humans have studied the humpback's song because it is so unique. You are also attracted by their white fins, which make them look like angels. Humpbacks sing with their head down. They do this regularly for 10-30 minutes.

You are fascinated because their song is the same everywhere on the world, in all oceans. Every year new songlines get added. But it is always the same song, in all oceans. That is how far our sounds carry, around the whole Earth, gently caressing Mother Earth and creating our light-frequency-grid.

Your scientists still can't figure out why we sing. The reason is that we sing our song for each other and for the Earth; we sing our love and wisdom. Holding energy, supporting planetary harmony and balance.

We are the frequency-keepers on Earth. We help our Earth evolve to higher levels, raising her energy level, preventing her from collapsing within herself.

Sometimes when some of you earthlings come close to us you feel nauseous, even have to vomit. It is because our frequencies penetrate you so deeply. They bring forth everything suppressed. This is cleansing so that you can find and hear your song, your voice again.

Our medicine is also wisdom. In us you find mirrored the wisdom that is also within each of you. It is wrapped in the great stillness of the deep, where we can hear the wisdom of our souls.

Water contains the Earth's history – we access it and send it out to you with sounds beyond your ability to hear but which penetrate the core of your soul. We are swimming libraries with the chronicles of the Earth – Earth's consciousness with everything that ever happened and ever will, all experiences and the history of the entire cosmos.

We are the libraries of the element water – just like the libraries of the element air and ether are the Akashic records. These carry the same information as we do, surrounding the Earth's atmosphere. The libraries of the element earth are the stones and minerals, the oldest on Earth. We whales are also amongst the oldest on our Blue Planet.

By providing different libraries of knowing, everybody, with different preferences of and connections to the elements, has access to this knowledge. Listen to us well.

You can also learn much from us about dreaming and about your dreams. Like our cousins the dolphins, when we rest, only half our brain is sleeping while the other side is awake. We have to do this to maintain consciousness to breathe because we are mammals, like you, and need to surface in the water for air. So when we sleep, we are in a continuous trance-like state and consciousness.

In this condition – just like you - we feel what is true, what is universal, all-one and connected. This way, you can also learn to use your brain more efficiently from us. This helps you to connect both sides of your brain, which is a cure against depression.

Give yourself time to dream. Don't just sleep to rest but also to dream, half-wake. It is in this state that you can connect with the matrix better than in any other. There, you feel the source and what your unique lifeplan and lifepurpose is.

Let yourself sink into the depth, fall into the deep, don't be afraid. You will find warmth, your home, connection.

We live in the physical yet also in realms of energy. We understand how to change domains and experience the world beyond linear time and space, entering many dimensions.

Our deepsea diving as well as our deep breathing of 300 mph or 480 km/h in half a second has a mind expanding effect. The material world disappears with us in white light stretching beyond three-dimensional existence. When you see us, you remember the source.

We represent your desire for wholeness as we dive into the deep unknown. Your thoughts go with us, the part of you open to change; your adventurous side, seeking truth, freedom, trusting in goodness, understanding and remembering.

Your essence receives our sounds and begins to resonate differently from what you experience in three-dimensional reality. We live in a holographic reality where past, present and future exist simultaneously, in which every configuration of matter and energy is possible.

The moment dolphins and whales disappear, you are aching in your heart for the source again.

Like the dolphins and you, we too are connected with the stars. We, like you, are star beings. We are not alone in the galaxy. We navigate by the glow of the stars as well as with the electromagnetic currents of the Earth which are created by the dynamics of the stars and universe.

When we arrive in the warm tropical waters to give birth to our babies and to rest, our cousins, the dolphins, are already waiting for us. We love being with each other. Like all of our kind we have regular large gatherings. We help one another. The dolphins are even midwives at our births. We live in a reality of peace, love and play, of harmony and communication.

Learn from us. Support and help one other, not only in your core family but also in your human family. We are all one family.

Let your heart sing, like we sing – then there will be peace on Earth. The outer world is a reflection of the inner world. Peace and beauty start inside you, so that it can also be that way outside. It means shining your own light and being joy.

In spirit, dolphins and whales are all one, light beings. Touch the star of light in your inner being, the crystal core in your heart, so that you may see with your souls. Ignite the true light of all humanity, lifting your spirits, lighting sparks of joy.

Find unconditional love and deep compassion and responsibility for Earth. Find peace within yourself and on our Blue Planet.«

29. Koyaanisqatsi – Crazy World

Finding and being at peace is challenging, as both history and the present state of affairs on our Blue Planet show. We are living in a time of great changes.

The teachings of numerous indigenous and ancient cultures, such as of the Hopi, Mayans, Egyptians or the Kabbalah, have always predicted times of turmoil. According to their worldview, such events are cyclical in nature.

There is a blooming of a culture, followed by a decay, then a cleansing and transition into something new.

The Hopi even have a name for such times of transition in their prophecies: *koyaanisqatsi*. This means a life out of balance, disintegrating and in moral corruption; a state of life that calls for another way of living.

What is fascinating is that, using astronomy, the Hopi and Mayan and other cultures were able to predict these transition periods in advance – thousands of years ago. Their scriptures say that we are currently again in such a transition and *koyaanisqatsi*.

The most accurate calculation comes from the Mayans. Their old writing says the climax of the changes we are now going through is on December 21 in 2012, within a 100-year-radius before and after this date.

I really wanted to understand why this is the case, so I undertook weeks of research. I am not an astronomer nor a physicist. Because of this, maybe I can explain in a language many people can understand.

There are two actual astronomical events taking place in the timeframe of 100 years before and after 2012. The first one is termed the »galactic alignment«.

To explain: Planets and sun share rougly the same pattern of orbit in our solar system. This is called the plane of the ecliptic.

From our perspective on Earth, the 12 star and planet constellations - known as the zodiac - line the ecliptic as the path taken by the Sun across the sky over the course of the year. Through the year, the Sun passes through each constellation in turn.

Over time, the Sun´s annual passage appears to recede counterclockwise by one degree every 72 years. This movement, called »precession«, is due to a slight wobble in the Earth´s axis as it spins. As a result, approximately every 2,160 years, the constellation visible on the equinox – December 21 - changes.

In Western astrological traditions, this signals the end of one astrological age – currently the Age of Pisces – and the beginning of another – Age of Aquarius. It is what shamanic traditions term the »Small Sun Year«.

Over the course of 26,000 years, precession makes one full circuit around the ecliptic. This is the »Large Sun Year« in shamanic terms and it is taking place in and around 2012, with an estimated 36-50 years before and after that.

It is not a sudden point in time through which the planets pass, but a process. This is mirrored by the development of mankind and its consciousness, reflecting the planetary movement.

For example, the Age of Pisces reflects compassion and forgiveness for others and self, represented through Jesus ringing in this age 2,000 years ago. Now, Aquarius is connected with freedom from all dogmatic traditions and an uprising of technological development – which is currently happening.

We are once again being liberated from the past; it is an outmoded concept, its attitutdes no longer apply. This time, traditional family structures are disentegrating to a more anonymous way of life. But at the same time there is the global realization that we are all connected. This is the next natural step to remembering and living that we are all one family.

The other astronomical event occuring in our day and age has to do with the band of the Milky Way, our galaxy. Every year on the winter solstice, the Earth, Sun and the galactic equator come into an alignment. And every year, the previously explained precession also pushes our solar system´s position a little further through the Miky Way´s band. Every 35 to 40 million years it passes through it to the other side.

To understand what the Milky Way´s band is: A galaxy such as ours requires a gigantic energy source to define the orbit of stars and planets within it. This »engine« is usually a black hole.

The central black hole in our galaxy has an estimated mass of over 1 trillion stars and can actually be seen as the great black hole in the center of the Milky Way. A black hole has such a high gravitational field that everything close to it gets pulled into it; not even light can escape out of it.

Old shamanic cultures say black holes are entrances to different dimensions and parallel universes – which is being confirmed by modern-day astro- as well as quantum physics.

A black hole spins at at an incredibly high speed due to its huge mass. Thereby it causes our galaxy to spin with it, creating it in the shape of a disk through its high spin. Most galaxies are flat and circular through this. The densest portion in this disk where the most stars are accumulated is called the galactic plane.

Our own solar system orbits around the galactic center – the black hole - of the Milky Way once every approx. 240 million years. Due to precession, it does this in a wave-like pattern, moving up and down through the galactic plane. It moves through the galactic plane every estimated 35 to 40 million years.

According to scientists at the Cardiff Centre for Astrobiology, this is what happened 65 million years ago when dinosaurs became extinct due to comet bombardment.

Gravitational forces from the surrounding giant gas and dust clouds dislodge comets from their paths. The comets plunge into the solar system, some of them colliding with the Earth.

The Cardiff team found that when we pass through the galactic plane every 35 to 40 million years, the chances of comet collisions increase tenfold. Evidence from craters on Earth also suggests we suffered many collisions approximately 36 million years ago. Our present position in the galaxy suggests we are now very close to another such period.

When exactly this will start is hard to estimate, because relative compared to the entire size of the Milky Way galaxy, its central plane could be paper thin. Thereby it might only take a few years for our solar system to pass through the solar plane and we woulnd´t know it until evidently shortly before.

We are in the midst of two cosmic mega events which take place every 26,000 as well as every 35 million years. Enormous physical powers are at work. All prophecies, such as the Hopi Blue Star prophecy, talk about this end of a cycle and the beginning of a new one, raising the Earth´s frequency and that of its consciousness, including humans. The world will go through a time of trial, suffering and purification before a time of one-heartedness. Then could come a golden age with humans at peace and a better life.

If this will happen acopalyptically or beneficially, say the Mayans and the Hopi, is based on the human decision of free will and whether enough people have formed the critical mass to make the jump to a higher consciousness.

Partially we have control over what will happen – but partially we don´t. We are really on a rollercoaster ride through time. Everybody feels the potential of destruction that is there. There is hope that this time we will be able to avoid atomic bombs and a worldwide war.

This alignment with the heart of our galaxy opens a channel for cosmic energy to flow through the Earth, cleansing it and everything that dwells upon it, raising all to a higher level of vibration.

Earth´s energy needs to be renewed, new ideas need space, body and soul need new challenges. The future has become presence and all dreams other than those built on prejudice have the possibility to become reality now. What is important remains. What is unimportant disappears and leaves.

Everyone is needed. You are not here for no reason. Everyone who is here now has an important purpose.

Filmmaker Godfrey Reggio named his award-winning and cult 1982 film after the Hopi expression *koyaanisqatsi*. In this movie without words, he shows images of the hectic Western world with music by Philip Glass accentuating the ever increasing speed and information flow of this day and age: millions of cars on highways, thousands of people rushing through city streets, the city glowing from artificial lighting. Pictures showing the hurriedness and soulessness of this day and age, the pointlessness behind the hurrying.

A world out of balance. People out of balance. People with starved souls. People chasing and running after something, without really knowing what.

Is it their soul they are looking for? Where has the soul gone?

30. Soul Retrieval

When I do healing work with clients, I ask them to imagine their soul as a bright and glowing ball of light. This lightball is what makes us alive and shine – our vital life force energy.

Over time, because of painful and traumatic experiences, parts of this soul energy go away. They don't disappear – because energy can never vanish. But they will go somewhere else and hide.

If your parents abused you, for example, or if you had an accident; grew up in harsh circumstances; where belittled at school – the list is endless – those parts of your soul hurting will leave you, because the pain is too much to feel and bear at that time.

A part of your soul may still be hanging out with the ex-partner you could never let go of; another part is still at the hospital where you had an appendix operation as a child, hiding in a dark corner.

If you experienced severe emotional or sexual trauma, parts of your soul may have travelled to a distant part of the universe, as far away as they could get, to hide out of fear. If you had an accident, part of your soul may have been whipped out of you, stranded somewhere, not able to find its way back home on its own.

The feeling of »not being here«, of somehow »not being complete«, comes from parts of the soul energy having left your core. In modern phsychology this is termed »dissociation«.

Humans try to compensate this missing life-force energy with food, alcohol, television, work, drugs – they are futile attempts to fill the hole again. Soul parts missing is one of the main reasons for addictions as well as depression – both common illnesses in the world today. Waking up in the morning and wanting to just go back to sleep, even though this planet is so beautiful, has become normal – more so than being happy and alive.

Other symptoms of when part of your vital life energy is missing are feeling chronically tired, cut off from life, dull, or having repeated accidents and chronic illnesses. Oftentimes a person can even be too ill, too lacking in parts of his soul to be able to die; countless people vegetating in hospitals for weeks, months, years are in this situation. They are not whole enough, not at peace enough to die.

Not only humans lack parts of their souls – also certain areas of our Earth. These are stretches of land where so much pollution has ravaged, war raged, so many of Earth´s resources been plundered that when you walk there, you want to get away as quickly as possible because it is so empty, haunting and painful. You can sense the harm that has been done to nature, to the animals, to the people there.

Bringing back lost parts of the soul for both the Earth as well as people is common practice in indigenous cultures. For example, after an accident, the person will first be taken care of by the medicine man – comparable to our doctors. Next, the shaman comes to the patient to bring back the lost soul parts.

Modern-day psychology and psychotherapy have this function too; however there is a limit as to how far they are effective. People may understand their problems and issues, have analyzed them in depth – but still, their soul feels incomplete because its essence is still missing. The work all happened in the mind – not the soul.

This is why soul retrieval work is so effective.

A lady has come to me with her ten-year-old son. She has been to a number of doctors and psychologists with him, however none of them were able to help or could even find a problem. Yet he is plagued by nightmares, afraid to fall asleep and thus constantly tired and nervous.

I gently make contact with the boy. Then, I ask him if it is allright that we do this work together – whether he would like to try and find a way to sleep and feel better. He nods. I ask him if he would like his mother to be in the room when we do this work. He prefers her to wait outside, in the waiting room.

I explain the soul retrieval work to him using the light ball to explain it. He understands it well.

I ask him to draw a picture of his soul energy. As he does, I see that large portions of the light are missing. I ask him where he thinks they are. He says he doesn't know. I ask him if he would like to try and find out and maybe get his lost light back. He says yes.

In the soul retrieval work, as I guide him into the trance, he tells me he sees his father and mother. They are fighting. His parents separated when he was two years old.

He tells me he is sleeping and then wakes up in his cot. His parents are shouting, his mother is also crying. Then, he hears his father stomping to the house door, going out, slamming the door shut.

The boy says that he leaves with his father. I ask him if he goes with him physically. He says no, but his light soul energy goes with him. Out of his bedroom, out of the house, following his father. It is still there.

I make contact with that part of him and ask if it wants to come back to the boy, where it belongs. It says no, it wants to stay with the father.

I ask this soul part of the boy what it needs to come back home, to the boy. It says that the father should promise never to leave him again.

In the trance, I let the little boy talk to his father and ask him that. The father answers: »But I never left you! I had to leave your mother, but that has nothing to do with you. I am always here for you.«

The little soul part of the boy is very surprised as he hears this; he always thought his father left because of him. Now he is willing to come back to the boy who is very glad about this.

I ask the little soul part that has come back what it needs, and it says the assurance from both parents that they will never leave him. I tell him that I am sure they will both give him this assurance.

Later, after asking the little boy if it is allright, I tell the mother what happened. She says that she would never leave her son and that his father wouldn´t either.

After this, the parents have the assignment to tell and affirm to their son that their separation had nothing to do with him but only with them, and that it is their matter to deal with, not his. They tell him they love him; even though they aren´t a couple anymore, they will always be his caring parents.

I work with the boy two more times after this and with his mother a few times individually to get over the separation. Even the father takes one session with me. Most of the boy´s fear of falling asleep subsides soon after the first session, and after the other ones, almost competely.

In his last session, he draws his soul energy ball again: It is full and bright. His parents are feeling better overall now too.

Any technique that makes a person resolve issues and feel better lets lost soul parts come back; it needn´t always be shamanic soul retrieval. Massages, pampering yourself, going on a long holiday – these too can be exactly what parts of your soul need to finally come back to you.

31. Women and Men in Balance – the World in Balance

When I meet a person, I scan their energy field like a dolphin – I have always done it this way. I look if their soul is at home and what their energy tells me about them.

It doesn´t make a difference whether they are rich or poor, male or female, beautifully dressed or not dressed at all - I have learned that the physical appearance *may*, but often says nothing of who the person really is.

If a person is in turmoil or tranquil, ill or healthy also says nothing about their level of consciousness. The turmoil or illness may be exactly the emotional, phsychological, spiritual and soul opening the person needs to evolve.

Part of my own journey was like this. Since puberty, I suffered from severe monthly menstrual cramps. They were so painful that I wasn´t able to go to school or later, work for a few days each month, knocking me off my feet and into bed.

I always felt something was imbalanced in my body. But whenever I went for my routine checkup, I was told that many women suffer from this and that is how it unfortunately is for sensitive women. Because I never experienced my menses any other way, I grew up with the understanding that this is the way it is. I allocated that some of my girlfriends had no problems whatsoever, whereas some did to what the doctors said: that some women are simply more sensitive than others.

Still, the feeling remained that this was no explanation for my cramps. It just didn't feel right that I and other women had to experience so much pain.

I always felt and considered myself strong and healthy – except for these few days each month. I organized my life around them.

At the same time, I looked for ways to start feeling better and turned inwards to find the cause for these pains. That is why I started learning yoga, about healthy nutrition and about the psyche at a young age. These monthly pains were an important part of my being a seeker, opening myself to the invisible world.

It wasn't until I was forty years that I finally would find the clinical diagnosis for my pains I had been suffering from on a monthly basis for 27 years.

I wasn't able to become pregnant for many years and I went to a doctor, a specialist who had been recommended to me. He tested my hormones and after these were fine, said the only way to know for sure everything was allright was to do an operation looking into my womb. I agreed.

The doctor found the cause: endometriosis. When he told me that the day after the operation, all I could say was: endo-*what*?! I had never heard of this before.

Endometrioses is a condition 75 percent of all women suffer from. It is the most common illness of sexually mature women but nonetheless only little known. An imbalance of the tissues within the womb nearly always makes it very painful, chronic but not fatal.

The pain is not due to heightened sensitivity; it is real, caused by tissue imbalance. Studies have shown that women with endometrioses actually cannot to go to work several days a month due to the painfulness of this illness. The majority of women not able to get pregnant suffer from endometrioses.

It is usually only possible to diagnose this illness during an operation. That, in combination with a still widespread belief amongst many doctors that the period of a woman is meant to be painful, has led to this illness being relatively unknown. Many women who suffer from it don't even know they have it, like I did for 27 years. When I finally received a name for my monthly pains, I was relieved to finally understand my condition and that it was not my sensitivity causing this pain.

The healing I have gone through has let me understand not only myself, but also the way things are *koyaanisqatsi* and out of balance on our planet. It has also helped me become more confident.

When you have gone through a long illness, don´t look back on the suffering but on God´s blessing that healing was possible. Equally, when you have solved any type of problem, don´t look back on the difficult moments but on the joy of having passed another test in life. These become your proof of being capable and give self-confidence for when obstacles appear.

What causes endometriosis is as yet unknown by science, as well as how to treat it. Some researchers say it comes from modern-day pollution and hormones in soil and food products; others say it originates from unhealthy and dysfunctional family structures. I believe it could be both. It recedes after menopause due to a change in hormone levels.

What heals it best is pregnancy and birth – as if the whole process of going into motherly womanhood brings the balance necessary. 75 percent of women with endometriosis giving birth are not afflicted by it anymore afterwards. I can gratefully say this is also the case with myself. I now enjoy pain-free month after month.

Often, when I went through my monthly pains, I had horrible visions of masses of women being raped and tortured in wars, in families, in past history. Of women being burnt to death. Pictures of humankind polluting the Earth, drilling holes into her to rape her of her minerals, oil, of her inner blood and organs.

I believe this illness – as well as others - is a result of all this, manifesting itself in women across the planet to finally be healed. It is a reflection of the wounded feminine energy on our planet.

This mirror shows how female energy has been suppressed and exploited for the last thousands of years and how Earth Mother is being exploited. The female and male energies on our planet are out of balance; today men also are groping for a way out of rigid structures.

How to do this? The first step lies in awareness. Realizing this is the current state of affairs on the planet as well as in men and women. This already brings a shift.

Not pretending that nothing is happening – not looking away anymore. Looking at it, feeling, observing, recognizing and seeing it, honoring it in this way.

Out of this awareness follow the next steps that need to be done. Be it healing your own inner wounds or working in your environment to help bring it back into balance. Be it looking to heal unhealthy structres in your family or in your workplace. You know what you can do.

Gentless and sensitivity – that which I love about the dolphins and whales – are also keys to letting the divine feminine return onto the planet from its shadow existence again.

Earth, say the shamanic traditions, is a female planet due to its nourishing qualitites, as the Sun is male due to its heating qualitites. Female gentleness and caring combined with male strength, female sensititivity and compassion combined with male focused intent need to be in a healthy balance.

There is a wonderful Native American Indian story about White Buffalo Woman which tells about the essence of this balance. It is considered the most important story in the mythology of the Native North American Indians.

Once, there was a time of famine. The chief sent out two scouts to hunt for food. As the scouts traveled they saw a figure in the distance. As they approached they saw that it was a beautiful young woman in white clothing.

One of the scouts was filled with desire for the woman. He approached her, telling his companion he would attempt to embrace the woman. If he found her pleasing, he would claim her as a wife. His companion warned him that she appeared to be a sacred woman, and to do anything sacrilegious would be folly. The scout ignored his advice.

The companion watched as the scout approached and embraced the woman. A white cloud enveloped the pair. After a while, the cloud disappeared and only the mysterious woman remained. The scout's bare bones lay on the ground before her.

The remaining scout was frightened and began to draw his bow, but the woman beckoned him forward, telling him that no harm would come to him. She explained that his weapons could not harm her. If he did as she instructed, she would help his tribe overcome the famine.

And so it was. The scout brought her to his tribe and explained what had happened. White Buffalo Woman was treated honorably and in return she taught the tribe many sacred rituals, helping the people connect with the source of all and live in harmony , balance and abundance.

The question in this story to each person is: Do you exploit women and the divine feminine or not? Do you, like the first scout, simply take what you want without sensitivity to the other person, the environment, to the next seven generations? Or do you, like the second scout, honor and realize universal laws and balance? Do you take advantage of others? Or do you provide warmth, inspiration and nourishment on different levels to the people around you?

This applies to both men as well as women, because we all have both masculine and feminine in each of us. Do you, aside from your outer actions, honor the female inside yourself – or do you let yourself be exploited?

Everybody must answer these questions individually. There may be areas of your life where you are in balance, whereas in others you are not.

Patriarchy as well as matriarchy are structural systems which cause confused female and male energies. We are both male and female. We can play with this and be incredibly masculine or inrcedibly feminine or both.

The balanced sides of the female and masculine aspects are creative. They give birth – be it to a child or a project, to a garden or music. These are those parts of us which really carry through with something, talking and acting positively. It is the the light side connecting a person with his inner wisdom and that of the source. The actions of a balanced person are in accordance with universal laws.

32. Life Passion

»Only he who lives his dreams can quench his longing«, one of my teachers once said. There is intense suffering if you do not live your exact life purpose. And you know it. It is an indescribable pain of knowing you are not living your life well. You wake up in the morning thinking: »What am I going to do today, oh no.« Year after year, month after month.

It is not everyone´s life purpose to change the world. For some it is to just sit quietly in a room, relaxing, resting and living a simple life. You have to find out what it is for you. Maybe it is to make people laugh.

   The only person who knows it is you. Then, you have a sense of getting up in the morning and knowing what to do and feeling good about it. Your life purpose – you love it. It can be difficult and very challenging, but you know this is what you have to do. It is what makes you grow and glow as a soul.

The path to finding your true soul purpose is often thwarted by many challenges and even difficulties.

Often, it means letting go of your origin family, even of an entire circle of friends; losing or leaving your job, the life you´re used to. Don´t live a role others have composed for you. Sometimes saying no means saying yes to yourself.

It means letting go of distractions you have become comfortable with – but which you know deep down are not what your life is about. Thus it usually means leaving your comfort zone – everything so familiar, but oftentimes unfulfilling. Why is this so? Because it is not your soul purpose.

If you are not in an environment supporting your growth, it is holding you back. It is a reflection of your shadow sides in you – your own fears, your own inner judgement against yourself holding you back.

In each of us something is waiting to be created. It is the center of our life, even if we try to ignore it or talk it away. Often this something is covered up for many years, even decades, by fears, feelings of guilt and indecisiveness.

You may have the feeling of living two lives: the one you are forced to live but don´t want, and the one which you dream of. You can let both lives approach one other. And gradually your dreams win, become reality.

When we decide to clear away everything that doesn´t belong to us and don´t doubt our capabilities, then we can fulfill the task which we are designated for. It is the only possibility to live truly fulfilled and with integrity.

Then you arrive in yourself. All of a sudden you get it and wonder why you struggled for such a long time.

Difficulties and problems always look easy when they are solved. But a large step, victory is the result of many small steps. Instead of thinking why it took you so long to get there, you can be grateful and happy that you finally arrived there.

Be honest with yourself: What is your heart's true desire? Don't be afraid of your own passion, for it will propel you naturally and excite and invigorate you.

Make sure your career matches your true interests. Make an honest assessment of how you spend your time. List your priorities. Take a class or start a hobby that really excites you. Invest time and money in manifesting your dreams. Give yourself permission to go for it.

Listen to your dreams.

They'll activate the poweful eruption of passion in your life.

33. Swimming with the very big Whales

I am ready to swim with the humpback whales, a life dream. It is just a few weeks before my UN-lecture.

Part of my work with the whales, dolphins and the oceans is to help awareness grow towards the beauty and also fragility of life in the oceans and on Earth. For this, I am invited to speak at the United Nations in 2007 in the Year of the Dolphin, to give a 90-minute-lecture about dolphins, whales and peace in this day and age.

Ric O´Barry, the trainer of original »Flipper« who turned away from training dolphins to become on of the most outspoken dolphin activists, emailed me a few days ago. He wishes me well for my talk and has included information about the hence still little known slaughtering of dolphins in Taiji, Japan. Just a few years later, the movie *The Cove*, documenting his work protecting the dolphins in Japan, wins an Academy Award in the category »Best Documentary Feature«.

Now, just a few weeks before my UN-talk which I am nervous about, I ask the whales to help me with their great size and strength to have the power and wisdom to carry through these 90 minutes professionally and in their best interest.

Humpback whales are huge. They are the third largest whales on the planet. A humpback whale's heart is the weight of three human adults.

I can hear them singing at night, my house is close to shore. I also dream of them; they are calling me.

I walk to the beach in the morning, but see nothing. I sense they are there. When I enter the water for a dip and dive down, I hear their magical singing again. I swim to the surface and see one of them spouting.

»It is time«, I hear them sing. I take a boogy-board to rest on as I await their approach, and slowly start swimming out with it. I swim for half and hour, the water is deep here and I cannot see the bottom.

I envision white light protecting me and have asked the ocean mother for permission to enter her this morning in safety, to visit her beings in their home and livingroom. She has given me permission. I am safe.

I am hanging in the middle of the bay. Every so often I see the whales surface in different parts of it, but I do not swim towards them. They will approach me, if it is so meant. Excited, I await their arrival – and at the same time am deeply relaxed, in a trance. I feel engulfed by their vibrations in the water.

I reflect about the last few years, the encounters from shore and boats with the whales, the messages I have received from them and the dreams. One of the messages is, that they have also asked me to work with them healing people, as have the dolphins. I am always very careful with such messages, to make sure they are not my wishful fantasy thinking.

I am lying on my board with these thoughts going through my mind, and have not seen the whales for fifteen minutes or so. I have no clue where they are in the bay. Again, I wonder if it really is meant for me to be able to work with the whales. I ask the whales for a very clear omen, a sign, so that I know it is a yes – or no.

Ten seconds later, the whale appears just infront of me. It is the young one, the baby, and it swims even closer, I can almost touch it. It´s eye looks at me very curiously and intelligently.

I am in awe from this baby whale that has suddenly appeared out of nowhere in front of me. I feel an even larger presence – the mother must be nearby. I sense her right below the baby and myself.

I look down – and there she is, just a few meters below us, turned on her side, looking up with her eye. She is looking straight at me, checking me out. I can see in her eye that she has agreed with my presence. It is friendly and warm.

I start crying – it cries itself up from deep down in my belly, a loving and happy crying, and incredible relief and release.

»All is well«, I sense the mama telling me.

She is so huge, right below me, and yet I feel her gentle presence. With a flick of her tail she could destroy me – but she is simply gentle.

»Tell the people to be gentle warriors of light. Stand up for love and peace«, she downloads to me. »Like we – who are of the largest on the planet – gentle and loving.«

Her wisdom is so ancient, I feel the truth in evey word she says. I am still crying, such a relief, to feel what I have always sensed. It is like an awakening of an old memory.

It is a deep opening for me.

Our encounter lasts for about a quarter of an hour – the baby swimming close to me, then a little off again, then coming back again several times. Very curious and a very, very large baby. The mama always trailing nearby.

At a bit of a distance – I can only vaguely see his contours under the water – is a male humpback whale. There is nearly always a male whale swimming with a mother and a baby in the early calf's months. Scientists term these male whales »escorts«. I believe they are there to give mother and baby backing and strength, in the same manner when dolphins give birth. Male dolphins surround the birthing mother and her female midwives on the outside, as a protective shield.

After a quarter of an hour the whales dive and disappear into the darkness of the depths. I slowly start to swim back to shore.

Back on the beach, I give an offering of thanks to the whales and ocean mother and sing a song to her in thanks.

At home, I eat a large meal and lie down to rest. Even though I feel tired, I cannot sleep – my body is buzzing with energy and download information. It is time to dream.

I lay there, dreaming, integrating the immense energy and presence of the whales, for hours, all day and afternoon. I feel energy moving and restructuring in my body; sensations of peace, love, understanding; a deep knowing that everything is right and well as it is.

In the evening I finally fall asleep to the singing of the whales in the bay. The download continues working in my cells. I dream about the whales.

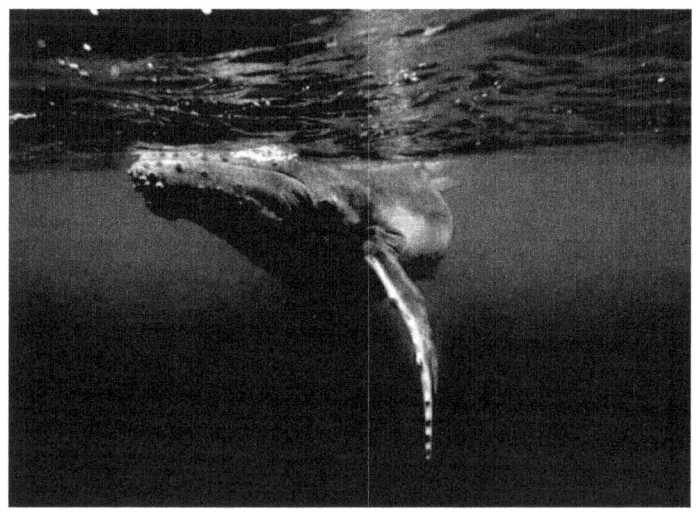

34. Dreaming

I am a dreamer. It is my strongest medicine ever since I am a child. Both my night- and my daydreams guide me – with clear signs and hints, also with warnings. Sometimes my ancestors as well as spirit beings visit me in my dreams.

My entire reality is »dreamt«; all my ideas, seminars, dolphins, life, this book – come to me through dreams.

Dreams are my most important companion and trail guide. They help me weave my reality with happiness, health, love, joy, and purpose in life.

Often my dreams are as real as waking reality, and what I dream occurs later.

I am dreaming, surrounded by dolphins. They swim all around me, enveloping me like the petals of a rose, a flower. I am in the middle. Pure bliss, joy, love. They are calling me.

I dream this several times, sometimes even during the day: suddenly they are there, all around me.

I long for gentleness and sensitivity and softness in people, as I have experienced with the dolphins and whales.

I travel to be with them again. The first morning I swim with them, I experience exactly what I dreamt.

Many people have these types of callings from dolphins and whales. It is wise to take these callings serious, to hear the message and medicine in them. Medicine is more than just a pill – it can be a cloud, or a tree, or an animal.

The dreamtime brings rest and recovery from everyday life so that other levels can surface. We can reconnect with the energy behind everything, the invisible world, the great mystery.

Dreams are wonderful experiences that help solve your problems. They can tell you a lot. Sometimes you can see the past and future in them. You also meet with people who have been part of your life or will be.

There are beautiful dreams but also those that frighten you. Nice dreams can show you where your soul traveled at night. Unpleasant dreams show you what you are afraid of. They make you aware of this so you can learn to dissolve your fears.

Dreams will never hurt you. They come to you as friends, to help you. When you tell someone your unpleasant dream, you will observe that your fear immediately becomes smaller or dissolves completely. Then, you will often have beautiful dreams. Dreaming helps your reality.

If you don´t remember your dreams after waking up or if they are confusing, that doesn´t matter –

because your soul understands these dreams and will solve what needs to be solved for you.

There is also a type of dreaming where you speak with God and the angels. You can visit them and live in their world at night. Sometimes you also work side by side with the angels and help beings in different solar systems who need healing.

The indigenous people most famous for working with their dreams are the Aborigines of Australia. For them, there is no difference between the dream- and the waking-state. The dreamtime is even more important and more real to them.

Regardless if you are awake or sleeping – the dream is the energy behind everything. It is the power which lives behind all visible things in the invisible world. It flows through all beings, it is the basic substance of the material world. The power of dreaming reflects in all things, it vibrates directly behind the everyday world.

In the beginning there is the dream, say the Aborigines. The dream creates the tree, the children, the spouse – everything. The ancestors dreamt the land into being. Aboriginal culture goes back 150,000 years of living peacefully with nature and the world surrounding it.

If you neglect dreaming, you neglect more than half of life, say the Aborigines. They meet to dream together, performing dreamtime ceremonies – all attempts to return into the state of the dreamtime. They go on walkabouts, which is a walk in the dreamtime – the same as the Indian medicine-vision walk, in essence. You walk in the invisible world.

In Hawaii, the day starts at night, because what is created and happens during the day originates from the dreams of the night. In the Hawaiian and other many old cultures when you get up, first you meet your family and talk about what everybody dreamt at night. You tell your dream to live in balance with life and nature.

The Senoi in Malaysia teach their children to complete their dreams. For example, if something frightening occurs in a dream, they ask the child to finish the dream and imagine a good ending.

When the child meets a monster it should ask the monster what gift it has for it. In a falling dream, they tell the child to fly in the dream.

In this way, the dream is not frightening and confusing, but beautiful, a wonderful part of life. This helps the child to understand the waking state as a continuation of the dream phase.

Every person can read his dreams best himself: How did you feel after awakening? How did you feel in your dream? This is usually derived from your life in the here and now.

Dreams are messages of the soul. Read the night's mail. You will find many answers in your dream. Also follow your daydreams.

Dream your life.

Let your dreams become reality in your life.

35. Children of the New Age

I am dreaming a past life. It is in an ancient time. I am a Buddhist nun in Southeast Asia. My head is shaven.

Being a nun fulfills me, I love it and am happy meditating and being there for people. We are living in peaceful times, there is no war and no severe poverty.

My home is in a large temple which also has an orphanage. The nearby forest is breathtakingly beautiful, there is also a river I like to sit at.

I work with the children in the orphanage and also give support and guidance to people coming to see me. The people in the area respect and honor me for what I do.

I grow to a very old age. I am happy – almost. What is unfulfilled in that lifetime is my deep wish to have children of my own; to go through the experience of pregnancy, birth and motherhood.

I wake up from my dream. My deep wish to have children of my own – I have had to be patient in this life too. Since I am a little girl, I know I would love to be a mother when I am grown. But the source has let me wait. Many, many years.

I know women who don´t want to have children, who have already had the experience often enough in past lives and have other things to do. But I am not one of them. I have always felt it would be a vital part of my journey, that I could give a lot to my chilren as well as receive and learn a great deal myself.

Whenever I ask my guides they say: »Patience, the children will come.« I should trust. And so I do, even if this trusting is often challenging.

In those years in my thirties, when many of my friends are busy with their new families – I am busy with my clients and students. I put all my nurturing, motherly and caring energy into supporting them on their journey. Helping them connect with the dolphins and whales, doing shamanic healing work, acting as a channel for any type of question they come for: work, soul purpose, love life, family, children.

Often I also work with their children. And every time, afterwards, I ask myself: When will my children come?

I am aware that through not having children yet, I am able to learn and grow in my spiritual work, in my life´s calling. Traveling, experiencing freedom and growth, gaining experience with thousands of people I support on the way.

But then, with forty years, it is enough: I know now really is the time; otherwise my body won´t be able to have children anymore, my biological clock is ticking.

It is in Hawaii that I pray deeply to finally become pregnant. I do a ceremony and cry, so deep is my longing. I am sitting by a small tree in a sheltered cove by the ocean where I love to go often.

I do the ceremony and close my eyes. My spirit guide is there and it is the first time that the answer is not: »Have patience – have faith – the children will come.« This time the answer is: »Yes, now is the time. You will be pregnant in a few months time. With twins.« They tell me their names.

I am so happy but at the same time doubt what I heard. What if it is only my wishful thinking and imagination that heard this answer.

»Open your eyes«, says my spirit guide. All around me are hundreds of white and yellow butterflies.

I see this, in wonder, tears streaming down my cheeks. Everywhere butterflies.

The miracle, the wonder is coming, very easily and lightly and gently like the butterflies. The miracle of a new life.

A new opening.

And so it is. A few months later I am pregnant. I know they will be twins, but my doctor says he doesn´t think so, it doesn´t look like it on the ultrasound. Still, I am certain.

A few weeks later, at the next examination, he says everything is looking good with the baby. I ask him to look again, if there might be another baby there. He shrugs, indicating he doesn´t think so, and turns the examination rod just to do me the favor. Then he stares on the screen in disbelief. There is another little one! Usually, he tells me, the mother faints when she hears she is getting twins; this time he faints, he says in amazement.

On my 41. birthday my belly is big and round with my little girls, identical twins. I feel like a whale, wonderful! A few months later my daughters are born, landing safely on Earth.

A new journey has started in my life with my children. I often think about how I can accompany them in the great mysteries and wonders of life. About everything that I learned and understand. I feel I am able to pass this on now with integrity.

I am ready to help each child develop a healthy consciousness and self esteem, so that they become self-confident and strong. So that they lead happy lives in abundance and material prosperity, with joy, spiritual awareness and love.

We want to safeguard our children from overload and estrangement. Again, I look to the indigenous people. People who have always attempted to live in harmony and balance with Earth, without completely exploiting, destroying it, the animals and nature.

Teach children from a young age about nature and natural laws. Talk to your child about the universe as the source and the Sun as father and Earth as mother, the Moon as the grandmother and the stars as grandfather and ancestors – then it will feel at home in the universe. Talk to your child about the Earth as a living being with a consciousness – just like you. It is not simply Earth – it is alive. As well as all the stones and plants on it. Show it that trees and plants and flowers can talk.

Tell it about angels and star beings, devas and fairies. Teach it how to see energy, how to recongnize an aura and how to use light and colors to protect itself. Show it how to feel what is good for it and what not so that it becomes its own authority.

Talk to your child about love. Play together, cuddle, be gentle and sensitive.

»Education«, coming from old Greek, means to »pull forth wisdom«. The children are waiting to recognize who they are, and you can help them. Let your child tell you its dreams in the morning. Watch its wishes, personal preferences, talents. Listen.

Ask it where it came from and what its plan is for this lifetime. What do you like to do the most, what can you do best and why did you come to Earth?

Help your child find its power animal. Let it connect with animals and nature.

Take it swimming in warm water at a very early age, to help it develop dolphin consciousness and awareness. My children have been swimming since they are two months. At their birth, because it was too difficult to birth twins in the ocean with dolphins, I played dolphin sounds accompanied by beautiful and relaxing piano music. The dolphins were there with us.

In the world that the children of the New Age are ushering in, we are more aware of our intuitive thoughts and feelings. More and more people are getting in touch with their psychic abilities. The interest in the paranormal is at an all-time high, accompanied by books, television, and movies on the topic. So, it is not surprising that the new generations are telepathic.

They are well connected to the source, communicative, and caring. They have been given the names indigo and crystal children, because they bring us higher levels of kindness and sensitivity. The indigo and crystal children and – meanwhile - adults are here to assist the world as we evolve to a higher vibration, where love and empathy become the norm rather than the exception.

There are also the star children. They are souls who come out of the future from distant galaxies to forward development. Often they are incarnated on Earth the first time and are not accustomed with the rules here.

Sometimes they don't really feel at home here. Things appear too dense, heavy and oldfashioned to them, too imobile, because they come from a lighter way of being. Their energy field is very high, bright and oftentimes almost cool. They are usually quick-witted.

They have a respectful manner, especially if one treats them that way. They often tell stories of foreign worlds.

Star children are not interested in family stories, religion, politics and history because they are thoroughly spiritual. The forms on Earth appear backward to them. They get bored easily. They are interested in astronomy and the universe. They follow their individual path.

Rainbow children carry old Earth knowledge. They are peaceful and strongly connected to the Earth. They talk with nature – rocks, plants and animals, as well as with angels and light beings. They feel energy very sensitively. They love being in nature. Oftentimes they are artistic.

Dolphin children love spreading joy and fun. They make people happy around them. They love the water. They enjoy communicating and moving. Thy do things playfully but clearly, and always as easily as is possible on the path of least resistance.

Their male and female sides are well balanced. They enjoy sounds and music, movement and dancing. They are teachers from the future, bringing new forms of communication and being, often telepathic.

We are in the ocean with dolphins. They are *jumping, swirling. They swim up to me, looking and gazing into my eyes, ancient wisdom speaking out of them.*

A young boy in my group, twelve years, loves to bodysurf in the waves. He is laughing, his eyes are glowing. I watch as a few of the dolphins surf with him. He is tumbling through the waves, but the dolphins never crash into him. Total body control, these magnificent swimmers of the seas. They all – boy and dolphins – repeat this several times.

As I watch them, I see the dolphins laughing with him. What a joyful existence, full of play and love!

Later, I am in the water with my small children. The dolphins are further out, waiting for when they are old enough to swim to them. We are surronded by several large sea turtles – honu, *as the Hawaiians call them. I see my childrens' eyes open in wonder and joy, they are laughing. The turtle – it is an ancient symbol for Mother Earth.*

May there be turtles, whales and dolphins, trees and plants to see for the children of our children in seven generations. May they enjoy the endless beauty and abundance on our planet, Earth!

About the Author

I was born in Amsterdam in 1968 and grew up multilingual in the United States and Europe. My upbringing in a UN-diplomatic family influenced me in being a bridge builder of different cultures and of a new age. I studied journalism in Boston and completed this enthusiastically and full of idealism with *magna cum laude* as second best in my class of 500 students. I worked in this field for 10 years: as editor for the magazine *marie claire*, radio talkshow host for SFB4 and freelance writer for various magazines.

At the same time, since I am 18 years, I am on a spiritual learning and healing path. My strongest influences were Sun Bear, Osho and Buddhism. Equally meaningful were and are for me being in nature, as well as extensive travels and encounters with whales and dolphins in the oceans of all continents.

I have been swimming with dolphins and whales since I am 23 years and had internships early with dolphin-organizations. I am trained in accompanying people to swim with free and wild dolphins; additionally, I am initiated in this shamanically. In my family of origin there are several divers, I am also a certified diver; that way I grew up with the sea and am experienced in the handlings of it. Safety of participants is first priority on all my dolphin- and whale-seminars. Thereby a relaxed contact with the ocean is possible. I feel myself to be a bridge-builder to the element water and the living beings therein. 2007 I spoke at the United Nations in the Year of the Dolphin about their protection and significance as ambassadors of peace and gentleness in our changing times.

I am trained in constellations and family sculpting, shiatsu and reiki as well as for sweatlodges and shamanic work. In shamanic healing I work according to the Core Shamanism of Sandra Ingerman (*Soul Retrieval*), Michael Harner as well as Sun Bear. This kind of shamanic healing is recognized by the WHO (World Health Organization) since 1980 as equally effective in treating psychosomatic disturbances as psychotherapy, as well as in the maintenance of a healthy balance of the four areas of humans of body - mind - feelings - soul. I was trained in constellations and family sculpting according to Virginia Satir, Bert Hellinger as well as energetic and shamanic methods of work with ancestors. I am also a certified Hatha-Yoga instructor.

Focus of my work are love, joy and lightness. Through healing the landscape of the soul everyone can find balance and the own and unique place in the mystery and wonder of life.

I am a happy and loving mother of two children

More information:
www.lisarainbow.com

Swimming with free Dolphins and Whales

with the author of
»The Opening«

LISA BIRITZ

www.lisarainbow.com

Image Credits:

Cover: © Francene Hart
Dolphin-Logo: © Design Lisa Biritz
Page 17: © Design Murat Karacay from the cover of the German version of Lisa Biritz´s book »The Opening« (»Spirit im Gepäck«)
Page 22: © Digital Creation Lisa Biritz
Page 36: © Lisa Biritz
Page 39: © Digital Creation Lisa Biritz
Page 50: © private archive Lisa Biritz
Page 59: © private archive Lisa Biritz
Page 71: © Roland Tonino
Page 87: © Digital Creation Lisa Biritz
Page 102: © private archive Lisa Biritz
Page 107: © Lisa Biritz
Page 121: © Lisa Biritz
Page 127: © Lisa Biritz
Page 137: © Lisa Biritz
Page 146: © Digital Creation Lisa Biritz
Page 165: © Wilfried Reiter
Page 189: © Lisa Biritz
Page 197: © B. Heagney & S. Frank
Page 209: © Lisa Biritz
Page 210: © private archive Lisa Biritz
Page 212: © Lisa Biritz, © B. Heagney & S. Frank

Lightning Source UK Ltd.
Milton Keynes UK
UKOW01f0351101017
310697UK00004B/145/P